Wake Up! Break Rules!

Wake Up! Break Rules!

IT'S TIME TO MAN UP & LIVE YOUR DESTINED LIFE

Charlene Gilman

Published by:
Executive Edgeworks LLC www.execedgeworks.com
ISBN-13: 9781533081162
ISBN-10: 1533081166

DEDICATION

This book is dedicated to the souls who have the desire and commitment to elevate their lives to new levels of success.

May you wake up to the inner calling that woke me up.

And to Connor Gilman, my loving husband, who provided so much support in making me see I had more value to share than what I realized.

CONTENTS

One

STIRRING AWARENESS

"You may control a mad elephant;
You may shut the mouth of the bear and the tiger;
Ride the lion and play with the cobra;
By alchemy you may learn your livelihood;
You may wander through the universe incognito;
Make vassals of the gods; be ever youthful;
You may walk in water and live in fire;
But control of the mind is better and more difficult."

—Paramahansa Yogananda

We have been connected for a reason!

You may be wondering what *Wake Up! Break Rules!* is all about. It's an awakening to the call of unfolding your true inner self. It's a committed way to becoming a fulfilled soul with purpose, love, and truth.

To be able to share your own truth, you have to get to know who you are first. Your mind can participate as either your biggest fan or your worst critic during this process. This book will share how it's possible to get your mind on board in becoming your biggest fan as you uncover your true self.

I used to sleepwalk when I was a child. One night I was sleepwalking, and my mother found me standing in the middle of the street with a car barreling down the road toward me. A Divine power was watching over me that night. My mother had heard my voice outside and whisked me away back to safety. I remember waking up to her panicked voice and not fully understanding what the commotion was about.

How many times throughout our lives are we sleepwalking, and the only thing that wakes us up is the hit? When we wake up, there is confusion and pain, and it's uncomfortable. We would rather stay in a zone with a sleepwalking mind-set, looking for the immediate and quick answers that will keep us in a sedate zone in which pain is minimal. As a knee-jerk reaction, our minds have been programmed to immediately enter into the zone of placing fault anywhere but on ourselves.

The mind will openly accept all normal information that we are accustomed to listening to on a daily basis: conversations with family, friends, and business associates; input from television and media; and the voices within our minds.

When we take one step that is out of the norm, our minds will perk up and say, "That's not normal!" When this red flag is thrown, fear kicks in and pulls us back to a safe zone. Our minds settle back into the lazy state and resume the usual dialogue in our heads. Our minds will resist the wake-up call as long as we allow them to.

Meanwhile, our inner truths are patiently waiting to be released. They have more power than what is showing up in our lives today. But they're not easy to unveil after years and years of sleepwalking through life. The calling is here to harness courage, confidence, and tenacity to control the mind to step in to a new state of awareness.

AWAKE MUCH

When and where did we pick up the habit of having so much worry and anxiety around living life? It seems we easily accept this state of mind without taking the time and making the effort to fully resolve the issues that keep us up at night. We go through the day filled with tasks to complete, but do we ever stop and ask why we are doing what we're doing?

Anxiety and fear sum up to be the main drivers that keep us going but at what cost? The costs are as follows:

- declining health,
- destroyed relationships, and
- large amounts of debt.

These silent killers of many people are limiting the vision of true wealth that is available for everyone to experience. It takes time to peel the layers of advice and teaching that have anchored us down. To unveil who you really are takes trust and courage. You must be willing to believe in yourself to the core to see your true beauty.

Instead of being awake due to anxiety and fear of the unknown, become awake in your day-to-day life of supreme bliss. To be awake means you are responsible for your actions, you are responsible for your results, and you have the courage to keep moving forward in life.

THE JOURNEY

My story is pretty common. I come from a lower-middle-class family. I was always taught that if you want it, you have to work for it. My parents, however, did not quite live up to their own words of advice. It was hard for me to capture the full understanding of their advice when it did not match their own actions.

For many years, I held grudges against those who had it easier than me, or so I thought. I did not know or give credit to the journeys of others because I was too busy playing the comparison game. I didn't understand why so many challenges came my way and why I was so resistant to them. I was so negative when I was seventeen years old that I had a car that would always break down when I drove it. My father would drive it, and the car would run just fine!

About thirteen years later, I decided to make some major changes in my life and focused my attention on developing me and my mind-set and on learning a new way of life that was foreign to me. I started reading more books and listening to people who were in alignment with my goals and focus.

By my own experience, I have found that in the moments when I drop the walls that keep me safe (too safe at times) and release the fear of judgment of what others will say, new opportunities appear all around me.

I began the mission of looking at all areas of my life that I wanted to work on. I figured I would start with areas that felt heavy on my heart. There were two such areas: career and relationships.

CAREER

I had so many questions around the methods I was following to climb the corporate ladder. What didn't make sense to me was seeing how bleak the leadership talent pool looked during my climb. I was fearful to think I would have to trust someone above me to have a level of control over my growth, all because they held a title that implied seniority. I knew I was capped at the glass ceiling. It was up to me to have the courage to utilize talents that I excelled in and continue my career development in alignment with my goals and focus.

RELATIONSHIPS

I did not grow up in an environment that provided an example of what a healthy relationship looks like. As I grew into adulthood, I struggled with relationships. One thing I did realize was that my parents and siblings had showed me what a relationship should not become. I had somewhat of a compass on this relationship thing, but I did not know where to start to develop a healthy one. So, I made myself a case study to see what I did well and did not do well in a relationship and to determine areas of my mind-set that needed further development.

When I started the journey of tearing down my personally developed beliefs around my career and relationships, I became committed to designing new life standards that would be flexible to my various stages of growth. For example, I had to determine the level of risk I was willing to take when I decided to start up my own consulting and coaching firm. I needed to determine areas in which I required more education and where I was going to obtain that education. At the beginning of this venture, I was a sponge taking in as much information as I could. But I was failing to implement the vast amount of information. I had to slow down. Being flexible in this process meant I would have to decipher which pieces of information would stick in my development and which pieces would not make the cut during that time.

QUESTIONABLE ADVICE

We are blessed to be in an environment of knowledge and intelligence that can help us move forward in life. In my journey, I have found many people who were willing to offer up their advice with the hope of and for the sake of changing someone's life for the better. The change lies within the perception of the person (me) receiving it and the implementation of the advice.

I have learned to question during the implementation phase how the advice will fit in with my current set of life standards. If it does not fit properly, I will question whether there is anything I need to change on my side to implement, because there are times where I have outgrown my goals and need to elevate into another set of goals. If there is not a fit on either end, I will dismiss the advice. But when I find advice that fits, I look to make changes and take the calculated risk on implementing.

WASTED DREAMS

Have you ever had someone tell you to get your head out of the clouds and that daydreaming was a waste of time? I have always been an avid daydreamer. I loved to think about the possibility of having a blissful life. In my distorted reality, I struggled with believing that I could actually have a blissful life. I held myself back; I took very limited action to make my dream come true. Instead, I decided to follow the masses of the population around me and shove my dreams aside.

This created a huge conflict within me. I could not understand why I was having the dream of wanting more and why I was not settling for less in my life. This inner conflict made me so uncomfortable that I built a wall of guilt over desiring more in my life. Who was I to think I could go for more than what I was accustomed to?

When I looked around, I saw so many people in pain, ranging from my parents to friends to big-name stars. So I settled for the status quo for a little while. Then I became jumpy to find a different viewpoint. I had a deep inner calling to keep searching. As I started to ask different questions of myself, I began to see a more successful pathway to making my dreams more of a reality.

MAN UP—YOU HAVE IT ALL

It's Time to Man Up and Live Your Destined Life. I had many people cringe once they read the subtitle to this book. They were hung up on the word *man*. I was glad to see them cringe because I knew I was making them feel uncomfortable. They were showing me how they get hung up on making judgments at a surface level instead of digging deeper.

The word *man* means "person or a male human," and *woman* means "female human." The critics' perceptions allowed them to go straight for a negative meaning and create an immediate belief that this book is sexist and speaks to a specific gender. If this is you, close the book now and gift it to someone who has the true courage and love for themselves to make some long-lasting life changes.

The underlying intention of this book is to drive you to a new level of awakening and shift you into taking life leaps through courage. If you read this subtitle again and connect it with the name of this book, *Wake Up! Break Rules!,* your perception will change. You will be in an empowered state in which you can take on the courage to harness the responsibility to have it all in life.

We all have everything we need to become balanced, wealthy, loving, and full of energy to take on more responsibility. It takes a deep inner commitment and self-trust to look for the underlying messages instead of placing judgement based on what is visible at the surface.

I often struggled with tapping into the idea of having it all. It didn't seem possible to go for big goals without thinking

I would lose control of who I thought I was. As I began to peel the layers, I started to see a light within me of a person I should get to know.

Here's what I mean. As soon as we are born, we arrive naked and screaming, and we get a good slap on the ass by the doctor to welcome us into this physical world. That is the first layer of another human's intention that's placed on us. Think of a lightbulb that has a frost coating on it. Each bit of frosting over a clear lightbulb is a hardened layer of intention from family, friends, media, television, or community. We lose out on seeing our true inner light. You can choose to be under the frost coating, or you can dive in and peel that frost coating off to be the true light you are meant to become. This is the difference between being unaware and becoming aware.

The energy that is developed in the process of peeling off the frost raises you to a level of clarity so that you can choose what you want to experience in life. You can take on more responsibility without feeling like it's a daunting task to even think about doing more. You do not become exhausted with the work and relationships you develop. You become a bright light to help others within your sphere of influence to uncover their lights as well. The thought of scarcity dissipates. The resources at your fingertips shift and change to become abundant as the layers fall off.

Two

BAD ADVICE

As a child, I was always asking questions. I still am today. Being a very curious soul, I wanted to learn, study, and experience as much as I could. But the people whom I asked questions of did not always provide the best answers or lead me in the right direction. It took me some time to sort through the misconstrued information to find my answers that connected with my life journey.

One example of an unhelpful answer I got was that I would not be successful if I did not have a college degree. I wanted to know what the direct correlation was between success and a college degree. Where did this belief come from? After receiving my MBA, it was apparent to me there was no direct connection between having a degree and an increase in my success. I found out I was taking on more student-loan debt, and I was reading more articles on high-level success for people who dropped out of college. Bad advice surrounds us each day.

This led me to wonder: is it bad advice, or are we asking bad questions? What are some of the main drivers that make us think it's truly bad advice versus our failure to dig around for more information? I have some answers:

- We stop being curious.
- We instantly believe what the news or media says.
- We continue to ask questions of the same person(s) or resource(s) consistently giving us bad advice.
- We have become lazy in doing our own research for information and news.
- We are closed-minded to new possibilities of elevating knowledge.

WE STOPPED BEING CURIOUS

I had a discussion with a family member about visiting me in Colorado at some point. He looked at me and thought I was crazy for asking him to come out. After asking him what was wrong, he responded with, "The state is covered in three to five feet of snow year-round! I am never going there!"

I laughed at the confident answer he had given me. I had to explain to him the seasonal occurrences that took place in the state versus those that took place in Texas. At the same time, I was amazed at how he had truly believed something his whole life that was not valid. The simple truth could have been uncovered by asking the right questions or by simply doing a little research of his own.

This example may seem to pretty simply uncover the truth. This scenario brings up a serious point, however: when did we stop becoming curious about everything and decide to trust and believe false systems?

We are in a prime time of being surrounded with plenty of information. The answers to questions are at our fingertips. Thank you, Google, Siri, Alexa, Cortana, and all the other platforms that share information.

Many times the safe, automatic default is to believe what we have been told in the past instead of taking the time to question it. If this is you, this is the wake-up call to get curious and question as much as possible.

NEWS AND MEDIA—FALSE CREDIBILITY

The news and media share information and tips that are trending based on what people want to hear and see. It's another form of entertainment that leads people into emotional states that offer only short-lived happiness and long-term fear. This acts as a shield that covers the ability of people to develop and live out their own truth. I do not blame these companies for the information they are presenting, but there is a different view to take.

Take the responsibility to decide what information you want to hear. Instead of turning on the channel and waiting for the news anchor to tell you what you should be paying attention to, turn off the news and research information that *you* are interested in learning more about.

To help me reset the flow of information, I did not turn on my television to watch the news for about six months. Instead, I received my news from friends and family. If I heard a piece of information that piqued my interest, I would go out and do more research on my own. In my own research process, I found that only half the story was being told. There were other pieces of information that led me to more research and more valuable content.

It's amazing to see how much true growth is going on around us every single day! I find it unfortunate that many people continue to live in a state of scarcity or are dependent on constantly hearing the same story: "It's a bad economy."

About five years ago, I wrote an article on how well the financial-services industry was doing and how much growth was taking place within certain sectors. Within five minutes of posting that article, I received a response from a friend, Nick, who was working in the same financial sector that I worked in. He was very frank in letting me know that my message was wrong and that I needed to double-check my data before making a claim of how well the financial-services industry was doing.

I jumped on a phone call with him because I was curious to hear why this article got him to respond so quickly that I was incorrect. After talking for a few minutes, I asked him if he had checked out Forbes 500 lately to see what was being reported across all US industries. That way, he could capture what was going on. He said he did not bother to look because "everybody" knew how bad it was in the financial sector.

I had a client, however, in the same financial sector that we were in that was growing rapidly and could not hire the right talent in a timely manner. Nick was quick to hang up and asked me to send him the link to the *Forbes* report so he could check it out.

What I realized from this event was that we believe only what we want to believe. We find an excuse for staying in a safety zone. My article made him uncomfortable because he was constantly hearing how bad the economy was doing, and then I offered up some information that was the opposite of what he wanted to believe. This threw him off his normal pattern of willingly accepting new information that conflicted with his current belief system. His sphere of influence kept feeding him information that he automatically agreed with, and he did not take any extra steps to research on his own. But to do just a little bit of work and research could open a can of worms that could actually change life for the better.

THE QUESTION GAME

How many times have you asked a friend or parent for some advice that ended up being the incorrect solution to your question? It's easy enough to push blame onto someone else who does not give great answers to the questions we throw out there. But are you aware enough to change your resources and ask better questions?

Growing up, we trust our parents and teachers to guide us on our life path. Then, we reach an age at which we start making our own decisions and may lean on parents, teachers, and friends. By the time early adulthood sets in, we are following the paths of those we surround ourselves with. All of this following around can do more damage than good for those of us who have a different path to follow and not one person in our sphere of influence who can push us in a direction meant for us. It takes courage and self-trust to break away from old patterns of advice and move onto a new path. It means getting out of your comfort zone.

When I was deciding to go back to school for my MBA, I knew I was going to make some life changes that would not please everyone. But I felt confident in my decision. At that time, I was managing a team, traveling to consult with out-of-state clients, training for obstacle-course races, and spending time with friends. Life was great, but I wanted more knowledge.

I kept my decision to start an MBA program a secret for a bit, until I was accepted into the program. When I announced my acceptance and my intention to start the program, I had a few people react with negative comments. These comments did not come from a malicious intent. Instead, they came from the fact that I was changing, which shook up their comfort zone.

I have found that the level of advice one receives will depend on one's own level of comfort with change. When the advice no longer matches one's "no-comfort-zone" style, people become uncomfortable and start to fall away.

The beauty is that there is no right or wrong. When people fall away, it just opens up more room, more doors, and more opportunities to seek advice from those who match my level of comfort with growth. The limitless answer shifts and moves faster and faster when you are more aligned with and focused on the way questions and answers resonate with the energy and momentum developed during this growth.

RESEARCHING INFORMATION

It's a prime time to seek information on just about anything we are looking for. So why do we trust all information received to be correct?

When I was taking the steps to start my company, I met a few people that said, "Most businesses fail within the first two to three years. You are going to have a hard time making it out there."

What a nice vote of confidence for someone just starting out! Of course, I researched this statement to test its validity. I was determined to not let this simple statement extinguish my passion for the results that I was after in my life.

When I researched the information, I found that the statistics at that time were valid. I resolved to not let that information stop me, and I was curious to see the other side of this lackluster answer. I also researched the successful start-ups and looked into what they were doing.

It didn't make any sense at all to listen to and believe only one side of the equation without pulling up some research on and articles about the fastest-growing companies of various sizes and in various industries. That's where I wanted my focus to be—not on the failed businesses!

I changed my search. I decided to look up "millionaire-minded people," and this simple search changed my life forever! I opened a world of unlimited possibilities and researched my way into a new lifestyle that the majority of people would only keep in their dreams instead of implementing and making a reality.

You have to think outside of what is normal for you and those around you in order to raise up to a new platform from which you can gather information. It is very uncomfortable at first, but when better answers and results come into your life, you will not dare go back to the old way of limited beliefs.

THE CLOSED-OFF MIND

"No!" is the knee-jerk response to statements that make us uncomfortable and uneasy and are not in the norm of how we think. It's the instant trigger to keep the comfort zone at status quo.

Ah…the peaceful silence.

NO! WAKE UP!

The closed-off mind keeps you in the same place with few-to-no results.

I was shy when I was young and did not want to play any sports because I hated to sweat. When the Olympic gymnastics session aired on television, I was inspired to learn to tumble and perform some basic flips. The opportunity came up to take it a step further and build more skills through cheerleading. I responded with "no" because it was my knee-jerk response. I did not want to push myself through an uncomfortable set of tasks.

I fought with myself over this closed-off mind-set for many years to come and within all areas of my life. Deep down, I had this dream to push myself and see what I was capable of accomplishing, but I had a fear of failure and a fear of success. I was driving myself crazy! I could visualize the accomplishment, but my mind was acting as a safety net to prevent me from breaking out of my personally developed comfort zone.

When I flipped this switch and decided to not be closed-minded going forward, the results came with bigger accomplishments. My curiosity took me in new directions with some amazing life experiences.

Small action steps to change a limiting mind-set will alter the way you see things. Instead of the initial "no" reaction, the response changes to a question based on curiosity. It's important to ask simple questions when breaking through the comfort zone. Ask simple questions, such as the following:

- What attachment do I have to this belief?
- Does this attachment serve my life today?
- How does this old belief help me in or deter me from the new goals and opportunities I am creating for myself?

REPROGRAM THE MIND
When I started the journey to reconstruct my life, I had to dig deep into the imprints and belief systems that were no

longer valid. I did not realize how much work and patience this was going to take. The door was open, and I gained a sliver of knowledge in finding my own truth. It was not easy for me to ignore.

Actually, when I tried to ignore the signals, I became more dissatisfied and irritated with myself. It's similar to trying to wear a favorite pair of shoes that you have outgrown. Trying to keep putting the shoes on your feet is too painful, but you don't want to give them up. At last, you decide to get rid of the shoes. The pain I am talking about is that pain of trying to move forward with your life using old patterns that no longer fit.

Curiosity plays a huge role in the reprogramming process, since it helps to keep the ego at bay. Ego will hold you back with habitual responses and reactions to make you believe it's more important to be right than to find your personal truth. When you become curious, you feel lighter and give yourself permission to make mistakes along the way. The little voices inside your head are willing to go along with you taking those steps, large or small, outside of your comfort zone.

We fall into the trap of thinking that once we are set in motion, the same old routine will suffice and there is no more growing that we should worry about. Here's a newsflash: we have been in this vicious cycle all of our lives. We learn just enough to feed our development during each phase of life. Then, we outgrow that model and *must* move into the next growth stage. Metaphorically speaking, what ends up happening is that we fall into thinking that once our shoe size has stopped growing, all other parts of us should stop growing too.

But when we remove ourselves from nonserving belief systems and release the resistance, we open up to constant life growth that needs new, elevated foundations. You should never get tired of this process! Those who do get tired of growth, development, and periodic self-analysis bring on stress and suffering by resisting and fighting a personal evolution.

As you focus on breaking down old beliefs that came from unfeasible advice, you will hear the voice of the person that gave you that belief. Acknowledge that voice in your head and break that pattern by saying, "Thank you for the advice, but this no longer serves me."

Come up with a new belief that resonates with you in that moment, and anchor it in by stating it or writing it down. The beauty of this process is that you remain flexible to the evolution of your new belief as you progress and continue to dig deep into your inner truth. When you dial in to your values, you will align to the personal beliefs within.

Three

CLARITY VERSUS CHAOS

When I switched to focusing on developing myself more, I had no idea what I was in for. Between 2009 and 2010, I became very curious to learn more about why I had a burning desire to not settle for the status quo.

This desire impacted all areas of my life, but I was in for a greater challenge than I expected. When I thought of my willingness to embark on learning more about this desire, I thought of the saying "Go big or go home." Well, I was already home within myself, so I had to make a decision on how big I wanted to go. I was tired of half-assing my commitments to change and felt a divine pull to uncover layers of fear and doubt that held me back.

The first seed of starting my own business was planted soon after that. I was attending a charity auction and ended up in a conversation between a group of business owners and investors. I was having a side conversation with one of the gentlemen in the group. He had a corporate background similar to mine and had started his own business two years prior to our discussion. I was curious to know what made him switch over to owning his business. I was intrigued by his courage and wanted to understand what drove him to take a giant leap.

Then, he said, "Charlene, quit your job and start your own business!"

The challenge was not immediately accepted by the voices in my head. By this point in my career, I loved what I was doing and could not picture much changing. Inner conflict and an uncomfortable feeling rose up within me. I knew deep down I couldn't settle for status quo, but I couldn't see much reason for change. Looking back, I now see this as a true example of listening with awareness in order to step up to a much larger calling.

I was so uncomfortable with the idea of a drastic change that I threw his comment aside and thought he was crazy for thinking I could do such a thing! On the other side of my thought process, though, I felt like I had just been given a life-changing seed and been given permission to act on something that would later become the best decision for me.

I was in a perfect position ten months later to act on my friend's comment, which I had not taken seriously before. But that seed was the catalyst in starting and growing my own business. It was not an easy switch for me. I struggled for five years to find my message, reprogram my mind-set, and study the experts within my field of interest.

I opened myself up to this process so much that I learned some high-priced lessons along the way. It was quite the journey to understand that I did not need to have so much attachment to something that I wanted to evolve. The attachment I needed to release was to knowing exactly how I was going to get to my bigger vision. I needed to be flexible during my transition and evolution phase while having my vision of serving people on a global level.

More chaos and mind chatter started to develop as I was transitioning into a new mind-set and life. Among my thoughts were the following.

- At this point, I was new to Colorado, and I was just starting to connect with a new community.
- I took a leap and left the large salary, seniority, and security of working for a large company.
- I was starting to learn more about what I truly valued in life.
- I had an opportunity to create a life that I thought was meant only for dreams.
- I had blindly stepped into a world of greater possibilities.

I realized that I took on quite a bit all at once for my life, and I do not regret any of the choices or experiences one bit. While going through so many changes, I felt overwhelmed and excited at the same time. In the back of my mind, I kept thinking, "There has to be a way." I just did not know what the way was! The uncharted avenue of my choices pushed me into taking larger, calculated risks.

The chaos that I encountered along the way put me on a path to making better decisions. Here are a few areas in which I started to become more curious with regard to how I was creating more chaos in my life rather than gaining a new level of clarity. The scenarios listed below are not meant to dissuade you from making your own personal choices on how you collaborate or gain information.

Mind-set shift: I had to heavily work on changing my mind-set from that of an employee to that of a business owner, leader, manager, and employee. There were many times when I was ready to fire myself due to a habitual employee set of rules. One of my problems was how to schedule my day of action steps versus work. I was still stuck with the guilty habit of an eight to five work schedule that took some time to break. I also had to learn not to take holidays off when the rest of the working world was taking that time off.

Networking events: I have experienced many people filling a room to hand out or obtain as many business cards as possible without the intent to find true collaborative and significant discussions. Or there's the opposite situation, in which people will go to an event, strike up a good conversation, never have a business card to hand out, and extend an invitation to attend a one-time, complimentary meeting of a networking group they run.

Networking groups: Many will not allow more than one person of the same category or industry to have membership in a group because they do not want competition. It's a waste of time to be around small-minded associates who are sitting in a cesspool of scarcity protecting themselves from competition.

SEO/Social-media experts: Many social-media experts are good at making new business owners feel like they are behind the times for not taking advantage of the varying social-media platforms. There are very few experts in this field who are interested in truly educating people on selecting the right media format for their needs.

Follow-up: Ninety percent of business contacts have very poor follow-up skills. It surprises me that these business owners are trying to run a successful business but lack the skills to follow up on the commitments they make in a meeting. It's no wonder why they continue to stay in start-up struggle mode or on the verge of failing as a business.

These are just a few of the experiences that I allowed to contribute to the chaos that I was attracting in my process. I realized I had to take a huge step back and get honest about where this chaos was taking me.

The chaos in my environment was pulling me away from my mission. I take complete responsibility for this and do not put any blame on anyone else. This chaos did move me into a place of clarity. It was only when I gained clarity that I was able to step up to the bigger mission I had envisioned for myself. This is a process in which it takes courage to be upfront and have a strong belief in your mission.

The following story illustrates what I mean. I had a high-end New York consultant who designed a program based on the strategies he had developed to make his own businesses a success. He approached me to see about connecting him with my contacts. The initial meeting went great, and we agreed to set up another meeting. I wanted to see him in action with his presentation before I introduced him to my contacts. The urgency he had to meet me, describe the education and expertise he delivers, and invite me to see him in action made me wonder if I was about to miss out on a good opportunity.

A few months later, I got to see him in action. He talked a big game to me about how he was changing business, and I was excited to see his expertly designed educational session. When I got there, I saw that he was moving his way around the room and talking to those who showed up. I loved seeing his interaction with his attendees. Then it came time for the presentation. After twenty minutes of a presentation on happiness, he wrapped up and quickly ran out the door. That was the extent of the education presented.

With my dialed-in focus on sticking to my standards, I had the courage to let him know of my dissatisfaction. I was clear and professional in letting him know the information presented did not meet the level of education and expertise that would fit with my associates. This experience gave me the courage to remove urgency while interviewing possible business collaborations.

The courage was a key to releasing unnecessary chaos and the fear of missing out. Many people will play on the fear of missing out to strike up a sense of urgency; they will make you feel that if you are not taking advantage of an offer, then you never will have an opportunity like that ever again.

I believe in letting go of this notion and taking the time to dial in to your values. Harness the courage to stand up and speak your truth.

Starting out, I noticed that I was getting a bad taste in my mouth regarding the process of building my business. I had to find a way to recommit and reconnect with the agreement I had made with myself, which was "I am on a mission to change lives for the better." I also had to understand what this meant to me and why I felt so strongly about this subject. The emotional pain that my family, friends, and business associates went through was not easy for me to turn away from and address with a simple "That's life."

What I decided to do instead involved getting quiet and asking myself what I must do today to get the results I am looking for. Also, I had to become curious about my mission. As a result, my meetings shifted to be more significant and collaborative on a deeper level.

What I mean by gaining more clarity is that you become more focused on where you spend your time, you value your time, you become more clear on what direction to take, and your conversations are more engaging.

If a new meeting is presented to me, I am not in a rush to add it to my calendar. Instead, I ask myself where and how this fits with the business strategies I am working on now.

When you get quiet and focused, the right people will start to come into your sphere. People will perk up with the intention to genuinely listen. The level of conversation will move to a new platform of true collaboration focused on results.

If you are dialed in to your mission and the level of service you look to deliver, it's important to not deviate from the set standards that you bring or an associate brings.

This is not meant to sound like a rant on the people you surround yourself with. But when you are looking to gain more clarity and focus, it is imperative that you become picky about the type of people you are attracting.

SMART PLANNING

When you mention the idea of starting a business, everyone becomes the expert on the first step to take. I had so many people tell me, "You have to have a specific business plan in place to even start. Who is your target audience? What businesses are you going after? If you do not know these answers, then you will fail."

I would like to give a shout-out to the naysayers who believe all questions must be answered before starting anything. They believe that if the answers are not there, then you cannot start the business or make a move. I find too many people get hung up in this area and never take a step to start anything. They use this as a crutch to procrastinate and make excuses for not taking action. These are the people that constantly say they are waiting for the perfect time.

Many people use acronyms with the word *smart* during the business-plan phase. I also find in this process that people will stop if they cannot perfect or find answers to their "smart" acronym. Why waste the time?

I do believe it helps to have a map or plan in place when starting your business. But if you cannot find answers to all of the matrices or to the "smart"-acronym exercise, this does not mean all hope is lost. It means you have more research to do. It means you should take some steps out of your comfort zone to find out what works and does not work for your mission. It means talking to someone who may have found success on the same path you are on.

When I think of smart planning, the word *action* comes to mind. You are not sitting on your butt waiting for all plans to be in perfect order before taking a step. You are taking actionable steps along the way and correcting mistakes along the way. The plan is going to evolve and take some exciting turns. The idea of planning opens up new ideas and strategies that are unknown to you but known to others. This starts to formulate a new wave in which you become an expert in your sphere of influence. You must ask yourself:

- What are the results I am after?
- What must I learn along the way?
- Who can help me reach my goals?

Business plans are not one size fits all. There are no special rules. There are no right and wrong ways of setting up a business plan. People leverage a variety of strategies and plans that fit the idea and action steps along the way. If someone designed a highly profitable system, it does not mean that system will benefit you in the same way. The experience, level of understanding, and commitment to implementation that you bring play a huge role in the results that you will achieve.

Define your own smart planning system that you are committed to implementing. If you wait around for what you deem the perfect time, it may be too late to gain any traction to move forward. Or you might allow any little unexpected life event, such as having to buy tires for your car, to be the excuse for why you cannot take that jump in life.

TUNE IN

Take the time to tune in. This means each day there should be some time allotted to getting quiet. Those answers you are searching for are coming from within. It's during the quiet times that the best ideas and answers have come my way. Sometimes we are in so much chaos that it seems impossible to slow down enough to be still. When we are in too much chaos, we start to make drastic decisions that move us further from our goals.

This is the time to relax and quiet the little voices inside your head. Release the worry, fear, frustrations, distractions, and short-lived excitements. If you are spiritual or have a god you pray to, this is the time to listen.

Too many times we fall into the chaotic flow and forget to reconnect with our own grounding source. This is the source that acts as our compass, gives us ideas, and tells us when to move. The chaos becomes so loud in our lives that we miss out on listening to the voice that gave us the set of original ideas to begin with. It's important to quiet our minds each day. Listen in to where you gained results, where there were mistakes, the lessons within the mistakes, and what needs to be corrected to grow into the next day.

I have found various techniques to help me tune in. As I continue to reinvent and evolve, the quiet and tune-in techniques change as well. Some people prefer yoga, meditation, going for a walk, or sitting quietly, to give a few examples, as ways to tune in. Find what works best for you in that moment.

Four

MIND AS A SERVANT

My mind has done an excellent job of playing tricks on me. I take 100 percent of the responsibility for this. For so long, I allowed the mindless thoughts and unhealthy emotions associated with them to help steer me toward a clear direction. Then I realized my mind was throwing me into a cycle of the same disappointing results over and over and over. My mind was out of control. This meant I had to put more focus on the types of thoughts I was having and figure out why I was spending time coming up with false scenarios driven by fear. I knew deep down I had to question it all. Prescription drugs from the doctor were not the answer.

We all have the power to make our minds work for us to better ourselves. Facing the tricks of the mind takes constant action and the commitment to do some deep digging, find a way to forgive ourselves, and love ourselves during this process. The main question to answer to get this process started is, how badly do you want to unveil the real you?

EMOTIONAL STATES

Emotion plays a huge role in how far you let your mind wander into scenarios that are not positive for your well-being. A perfect example comes to mind in considering the thought process involved in making a call to a family member. That process might go like this: "I need to call my sister today. It's been about a week since we last spoke. I will call her in a few minutes, after I finish this e-mail. Well, she kind of pissed me off the last time we spoke. I am not in the mood to have that conversation again. Forget it; I will call her later. I am not going to allow her to get me mad all over again." (I'm already angry at this point for no reason.)

At the beginning of my thought process, I was completely on board with catching up with my sister. Then, as I let my mind wander around, I allowed the emotion from the previous conversation talk me out of calling her. I fell into a pissed-off emotional state without even talking to her!

Since I have worked on my mind-set and started making my mind work for the better, I would now stop the emotional madness at "I will call her in a few minutes, after I finish this e-mail." My mind is only on when I am calling her. My focus is now back on the task at hand, and I step into the call with a different mind-set. This is a practice that takes time to get used to. I have been practicing this technique for quite some time. Now the negative emotional state comes up very infrequently, whereas it used to come up all the time.

Working on emotional states is different for everyone. I have learned that most people do not want to invest this kind of time in themselves because they are too terrified of what they may find. They prefer the prescription method to keep the veil on as long as possible. Do not get me wrong; I do believe prescriptions help alleviate symptoms, but they do not get rid of the actual problem that ignited the symptoms. We have to be willing to take a leap of faith to commit to getting to know ourselves so that we can remove those problematic roots in our lives.

MIND CHATTER

How many voices are going on in your head today? Think about it for a moment. Is the television on? Are you texting, driving, and talking on the phone at the same time? Are you in a negative state of mind that makes you feel like you just can't think?

Our brains are filtering so much information each moment. The only things we are able to see are what the brain has just filtered based on what you are looking for in that moment. Have you ever noticed that when you buy a new car, everyone seems to have that same car model? That's a filter the brain is looking for. What about the filters we have from old information that is no longer valid or serves you today? Have you taken the time to dig into any of these filters?

For many years my mother used to say, "Don't walk outside with wet hair. You will catch a cold." Guess what? For many years I believed that I would catch a cold by doing this. I thought I was a sickly child because I used to go outside with wet hair. Obviously, when I walk outside with wet hair today, my mind knows better than to believe an old statement that no longer fits within my belief and filter system. I have been able to stop her voice from saying that to me over and over, day after day, year after year, as when I was a kid.

The mind chatter can be controlled and shifted to a new state. The voices from the past can be removed and replaced with positive voices that are actually in alignment with where you are today.

Are you listening to the right voice? It takes self-trust and confidence to get quiet and listen to the quiet voice that often gets trampled by the other loud voices running through our heads. This quiet voice is the one that truly leads us. Every one of us has tapped into this voice in our lives. But we get swept away into the chaos that makes it hard for us to keep coming back to it. Are you willing to take the chance to open up to the quiet voice more often than to the other voices?

HABITUAL DOUBTS

The habitual doubts will keep you pinned in one spot for as long as you let them. My shyness as a kid brought doubt my way in just about everything I did. Those doubts were a detriment to the talent and energy that I had within me. Many times adults will say things to kids, and they do not take any responsibility for the damage they cause. It is highly unfortunate that the jealousy that adults transfer onto kids has caused more damage to the development of those children than they realize.

The top statements from adults that inspired habitual doubt in my adult life were these:

- Why aren't you as pretty as your sister?
- Get that trash out of my house; she is not white!
- You made a ninety-nine on your test. That's not good enough!
- Your parents never went to college, and they do not have much money. That is a sign that you will not have much, either.

As I child, I thought all of these statements were true about me, because I trusted my elders to know best. I went through life taking on what was easy because I believed I was not good enough to go much further than that. Imagine holding on to the most damaging statements in your life and adopting them as your reality when the truth is quietly telling you there is so much more to you that is to be revealed. We end up trusting random, damaging statements. The reality is that truth is in the subtle, quiet voice patiently waiting for you to turn your attention inward instead of outward.

I got to a point at which I had to stop listening to the outside world for a while. Who are they to know who I truly am? Even those around me who would say "I know you" actually do not know *me*. They may be in flow with my energy in that moment, but they do not know *me*.

The hidden, habitual doubts must be removed to get to know your inner self. That is the truth. I have learned to release the attachment to someone else's ignorance and listen in to truth that resonates with me. Once you start peeling these layers off, your presence shines brighter, your confidence is beaming, and the doubts no longer weigh you down.

FEAR

Fear is an emotion that makes us believe something is going to cause us pain or harm of some sort. Habitual doubt accented with the emotion of fear will shut down any type of life-changing decision. How many people do you know who will shut down an idea so quickly because of a bad experience they had the first time they tried it? Better yet, they just think something bad is going to happen, so they do not want to entertain the idea at all.

I had an opportunity to face my fear of the dark. When I was nineteen, a group of friends wanted to go rappelling off a railroad bridge at midnight. The idea was awesome to me, and I could not wait to go. This was my first time to ever rappel, and I was with a seasoned group who knew this area very well.

As we walked along the railroad bridge, I started to get scared and second-guessed myself for trying this new adventure. I was standing in the middle of the bridge, and I looked down. It was pitch black, and I could not see a thing below me. I backed up and started walking back to the parking lot. Then, I was halted by the guy I was dating at the time. He asked why I was leaving. I stopped, turned around, and realized I did not have a valid answer for him. I had a discussion in my head. I thought, Charlene, if you don't do this now, you know you will never want to do this again.

I wanted to face my fear of the dark, unknown territory that would become a new experience for me. I felt the need to give myself a chance to try something that was not in my normal day-to-day life at this point. I was harnessed in and given instruction, and I needed to trust the process. There was a team waiting for me at the bottom with lights. My first push from the bridge was scary and fun at the same time. I was excited to keep moving toward the lights below. The adrenaline rush of victory was an awakening! The team celebrated my arrival. I felt empowered by facing my fear and then instantly found myself cheering on the next person. I had so much fun that I could not wait to try it out again.

How often does fear make you feel as if you are about to take a journey into dark, unknown territory? How often has it stopped you from moving forward in your life, relationships, health, or career?

That glimmer of victory in the dark lit a way for me to take chances on myself. I gave myself the flexibility to face that fear. Instead of listening to all the red flags and alarms going off in my head, I made a move into the unknown darkness by listening to the quiet, subtle voice. I grew from that quiet space. It's those little steps we take to move past the alerts and mind chatter that allow us to slowly start to free ourselves from a cocoon that no longer fits us.

POWER OF PERMISSION

What rules do you have in your life today that keep you in a safe bubble? Do you know why you have those rules? Have you taken the time to observe and question the rules you have in your life? Are these rules helping you or damaging you?

The mind can be a wonderful servant for you if you train it to give you permission to venture out of your comfort zone. It actually needs direction from you. If you sit on autopilot, your mind will give you answers and direction only based on your past habits, filters, and beliefs. The mind is unable to give you more than that. It is only when you wake up and become alert that the mind will clue in that something is changing. Consider the following scenario.

Kim: I am tired of my current career. I want to do something new that will challenge me.

Her Mind: You're too old for a new career.

Kim: I am stuck, then, in a dead-end job. Where did I go wrong?

Her Mind: Don't change anything. Maybe you will get a raise.

Kim: I guess these are the cards I was dealt in life.

This example is classic to the majority of people not giving themselves the permission to trump the mind and develop a new way of thinking. Here is how the conversation in Kim's mind should go if she is to break its autopilot responses.

Kim: I am tired of my current career. I want to do something new that will challenge me.

Her Mind: You're too old for a new career.

Kim: I am sure I am not the only one wanting to make this type of change at this point in my life. Maybe there are people out there who have done this.

Her Mind: Don't change anything. Maybe you will get a raise.

Kim: I need to do some research on this. I would like to make a plan for how to change my career. If I get a raise anytime soon, that would be awesome, because then I can use those extra funds for research and education if needed.

Her Mind: OK, give it a shot.

Kim has given herself the permission to not allow her autopilot mind to have control. Instead, she moved past the original negative thought. She found a way to make it a plus if she got the raise, but she was still focused on the commitment to change her career.

The autopilot mind will respond and jump on board when you are strong enough to break the normal thought patterns. The more you practice this process, the more the mind will settle down and not throw false red flags. You will become more aligned with your inner calling. Give your mind a break, become more curious, and have fun trying new experiences that are of interest to you.

GOLDEN KEY

Mind-body-health expert Laura Stout shares her story of how she took the reins over her mind to commit to a new, healthy lifestyle. She hit her limit of having health problems at a very young age and took control of her mind to get on board with her heart's desire.

Char: What was your experience on the day of awakening to a healthier lifestyle?

Laura: I was in the dressing room of a department store and could not fit into a size-14 outfit. This was my limit, and reality struck hard to make some changes in my life.

Char: What was your first step?

Laura: All my life I had struggled with my weight, stomachaches, and digestive issues. I grew up in an Italian household with lots of pasta and bread. I had no idea that my issues were related to the food I was eating. I made a small shift in my diet by eliminating grains and eating more vegetables. I stuck with my normal workout routine as well.

Char: How did this small switch impact your health?

Laura: I lost fifty pounds quickly. Then, later on, I found out I was gluten intolerant.

Char: What was going on with your mind-set during this shift?

Laura: My mind struggled with thinking I was still a fat person, and I needed to reprogram my brain. I struggled with this mind-set for ten years after losing the fifty pounds. My subconscious mind was still stuck in an old pattern.

Char: How did you break this pattern to shift your mind to be on board with your body today?

Laura: I started learning about self-development through a network marketing company that I was introduced to. This was huge for me!

By retraining my mind, I was able to let go of foods that no longer fit my body type. My thoughts have shifted to a new way of thinking about what I am putting in my body as fuel. Am I feeding my body with nutrients or crap?

I now train clients on my personal system and workshop that has helped me sync my mind with my body. This program is called MEDS, which stands for meditation, exercise, diet, and sleep.

It makes a huge difference to pay attention to the foods you consume. The impact shows up in your level of energy, mind-set, and choices you make on a daily basis.

Char: Where do you have your clients start?

Laura: I help my clients define their "why" based on why they choose to have a healthy lifestyle. If they are going to create new habits, they must have a good understanding of why they have bad habits today. For example, people will eat a whole bag of chips while they are watching television. They are performing unconscious eating while doing a mindless activity.

I train my clients to stand strong in making sure they are not doing this for anyone else but for themselves.

Laura's Take Action Today

- When starting this journey, find like-minded people on your same journey who can support you.
- Find a support system to keep you honest in your transition.
- If you come up against resistance from loved ones, ask them: why can't you support me in being healthy?

Break the Cycle!

Family members in poor health are a wake-up call to shift your lifestyle to choose to be healthy. Take control and make the shift to educate yourself on how to take the steps for a lifestyle change.

Five

DECLUTTER RELATIONSHIPS

I spent so many years thinking I knew what it took to create a healthy relationship. But I was doing more damage than good. When I dropped the mask of pride and decided to show up with the very few relationship skills that were working for me, I created the space to learn new relationship skills. The reward that I've received from facing my truth has been so sweet that the negative baggage from past relationships has melted away.

No matter how hard I fought with my ego, I had to dig deep to find the strength to honestly speak my truth to my husband. I said to him, "I don't know what a healthy relationship looks like, but I want to create a way to have a healthy relationship that works for both of us." That statement caused a huge shift in my life at that moment. It took years and years to get to a point at which I could stand in vulnerability and trust that this statement would not change his love for me.

GET TO KNOW YOU

Have you met someone who cannot be alone? This person has to have constant interaction or constant noise going on. These are people who cannot fall asleep without having their televisions blaring in the background and playing all night. They are so terrified of the silence and of being alone with their own thoughts.

The quiet alone time is one of the wealthiest times to have, even if it's just for five minutes in the morning and five minutes in the evening. This is when being honest with yourself is crucial. The truth that lives within you will start to appear, and you will start to see what changes should be made in your life to get in alignment with your destiny.

When I started committing more time to getting to know myself, I started asking so many questions. I was eager to connect with my values. It was also a time for me to be honest about why certain types of relationships had failed.

- Career relationships had failed because I was serial job hopper for many years and burned bridges along the way.
- Romantic relationships had failed because I was a serial dater and burned bridges along the way.
- Family relationships had failed because I attended family events only when asked to appear.
- My relationship with myself had failed because all I did was work out, climb the corporate ladder, and study. I was interested only in quick and easy results.

The common denominator in all these subpar relationships was *me*. Yes, I could have taken the easy route of pushing blame onto others for things that were not working. The blame game gets old pretty quickly, though, and I became tired of hearing myself with the same set of excuses. Also, after a certain age, you have to take full responsibility for yourself. If I am tired of it, others around me are tired of it too! Something had to change. That meant me.

This first step included me writing down the answers to the many questions I had about my values, but I had to get quiet. The background noise of the television and phone had to stop for a while. Since this was new to me, it took some time to clear the chatter out of my head that was making me think I was going to miss some earth-shattering news if I turned off the technology.

The relationship with myself was the starting point for improving any other relationships in my life. You may be familiar with people saying that you have to help others before you help yourself. This statement causes so much guilt and anger. By taking a good look at this statement and seeing the trail of failed relationships in your life, you can see that an important ingredient is missing. To be in a place of helping or in a place of developing a good relationship, you have to know how to have a good relationship with yourself. Then, you can apply those successful ingredients to other relationships.

If you start taking the time to have quiet alone time, release yourself of any guilt that comes up in getting to know who you really are and what you value. Give yourself permission to fall in love with yourself!

BREAKING BAD RELATIONSHIP CYCLES

Have you ever noticed that you attract the same bad relationships over and over? Sometimes you may feel that this is just what life is going to hand you and that you might as well pick the lesser of two evils.

When I was working for a financial fixed-income company in Dallas, I spent time on the road consulting with the big financial firms in New York, San Francisco, and Houston. When I was not on the road, I was managing a team, studying for my MBA, and training in CrossFit. My time was filled with things to do, but there was no personal relationship. I was also tired of the cycle of bad relationships.

One day I was having a discussion with a dear friend who was listening to my pity party on not being in a relationship. The conversation went something like this:

Me: I don't think I will ever find a man.

Friend: You will never be able to have a relationship being on the road all the time. Plus, you have already built your life, and you have everything you could ever want. There is no man that would be able to handle you.

Me: Maybe you are right, but I don't believe that statement. I just have to figure out a way to make it work. I am tired of the wrong man coming into my life.

Deep down, I knew truth was being delivered underneath the words spoken. I also knew I had to be the one to find my way. On top of this, my ego was fighting with the surface-level words spoken to me in that moment because I did not want to be wrong. It was time for me to be honest and listen to the truth. I had to get ready to do some work on myself. I knew that if I wanted it, I would have to step up my game in building a relationship with myself so that I could know what I wanted in a relationship and not compare myself to my friends and their relationships.

I realized I became tired of the relationships that did not work, and I knew it was not the time to keep doing the same routine over and over thinking the right relationship would just land in my lap. This meant that in order for me to build and find the right relationships on all levels, I had to stop the cycle and ask questions:

- What is the common denominator in relationships?
- What and who do I attract in my life that is not a fit for my standards?
- What must I do to no longer deviate from my standards?
- Who fits my standards today out of my friends, family, business colleagues, and significant others?

These are the questions that I started asking to build the types of relationships that I knew deep down would be in alignment with my values.

When you write out the essence of the type of relationship you would like to surround yourself with, you will begin to feel the shift in conversations and people you attract. The old relationship cycles start to move away from you, and you start to see true quality from a different viewpoint. Things that may have bothered you about someone before are no longer important. Instead of picking out what you don't like about a person, you start to determine whether a person matches your values and the essence of what the person brings to the table. If there is no match, the egoistic response is released. You let it go and move on to the next level in building your relationship foundation. You stick with your relationship standards with more confidence because you *know* those relationships exist.

OLD HABITS

What showed up for me in the process of decluttering relationships were the many bad habits I had imprinted in my mind and belief system from years of witnessing and being around poor relationships. My parents had a very volatile relationship, and there were many things I was repeating in my own life that mirrored their behavior and relationship style.

What about the baggage from previous relationships? Along the way, we pick up bad habits and behaviors from those we have surrounded ourselves with in work, social, and family environments. All the gossip, negative statements, negative reactions, and invalid perceptions get locked into our own ideas of what life should be like. We let go of our own inner truth and values just to fit in with the social comfort zone of what others value.

Behind closed doors, the social mask must fall away, and we have to fight the guilt of not living our own truth that day. Sometimes the pain is too hard to face for some, and they unfortunately become dependent on antidepressants, only to feel numb when they are alone. The key is to be in your truth at all times to the best of your ability.

One by one I had to chip away at the negative blocks to dig into what I envisioned would be a healthy relationship. *People* magazine was not a resource that I depended on for this venture. I had to remove myself from any type of outside influences. I am grateful I had the mountains close by to hike, connect with nature, and self-analyze using the following questions:

- Where am I falling in short in relationships?
- What are some of the old habits that no longer serve me today?
- How can I implement and replace the old with a healthier new?
- Why do I feel a sense of attachment to this habit?
- What is my intention of the day to stay true to my relationship standards?

Along with these questions came another realization: that it was time for me to get rid of any material items that had emotional anchors that were no longer serving me today.

Old habits make us want to hold on to material things with some emotional attachment that we want to associate with the memory. This is of no service when you are elevating your relationship foundation to align with your values. The purge of materials opens the space for a purge of emotions.

I am not suggesting you go through your house and trash everything you own. But you know what you are holding on to that goes against your relationship values and the standards that you are building in your life today. Be honest and true in the purging process.

TRUST FOUNDATION

I often find that lack of trust is the main reason that relationships end. People have ideas of how relationships should be, and they become controlling of others' perceptions, thinking that is how trust is built.

Consider the following scenario, in which lack of trust gets way out of hand:

Jane finds a new Netflix show that she wants to binge-watch as time permits.

Jane's boyfriend, Bill, likes the show and wants to watch it as well.

Somehow an agreement is made that Bill is not allowed to watch the show without Jane and vice versa. Yea! All is well; Bill and Jane have a show to watch together. They have now created an agreement that does not bring quality to their relationship.

One day, Bill has some spare time and decides to watch the next episode of the show.

Blasphemy! Jane finds out, and she is fuming mad that he watched the next episode without her. This was the last thing that could have happened on a bad day. How dare he do such a thing!

Jane instantly starts yelling at Bill; she says she feels betrayed and can no longer trust him. Then she brings up that time when there was that incident that made her lose trust in him. But she realizes that was the wrong guy in that story. Oops! She got Bill confused with someone else. Angry Jane then brings up another story in which Bill was actually there and did something wrong to reduce the level of trust.

This is an example of pure madness in which people hold on to small issues that have no bearing on relationship quality or value. The lack of trust cycle continues until you are ready to stop the madness. Learn to trust yourself *first*. When you develop your relationship values, you must be the student first. The most important lesson based on Jane's scenario: do not create a prison for yourself!

Deciding who can watch a show with or without you is sheer lunacy. And why would you want to spend your time getting pissed about something that has no value to your life and relationship? Instead, focus on turning off the television and having a conversation without distractions. Get to know the person sitting next to you.

Each night my husband and I take about thirty minutes to an hour discussing our day. In the first year of doing this exercise, I have realized the following:

- He has his own life journey and experiences.
- He is showing me his own personal truth of how the day has impacted his life and perceptions.
- I get to share my own life journey and experiences.
- I get to show him my own personal truth of how the day impacted my life and perceptions.
- We openly discuss ideas or other ways of looking at the experiences.

We both have a valuable discussion and add a new layer to our relationship foundation. We are building trust within ourselves and within each other by being our true selves. This exercise is a process that helps you to stand in your own truth each day with the knowledge that this can be shared in a safe and trusting environment.

DECLUTTER PROCESS

The process of decluttering people from my sphere of influence was very hard to start. But I found a method to this process that was effective.

Several years ago, I was sitting in a conference, and the speaker was talking about how he removed people from his circle. He decided to go through his cell phone and remove contacts that he had not spoken to for over a year. His technique resonated with me, and I knew I had to take action in cleaning up my contacts. That night I removed sixty phone numbers from my cell phone. It was hard at first because my mind chatter kept creeping in with, "What if this person calls me, and I don't know who it is?" Or it would ask, "What if I need to reach this person at a later time?"

I discarded those statements and continued the process. I realized that if I needed to get in contact with someone who was being removed, I could easily find them on some social media platform. Now I clean out my contacts about every six months.

The next step I had to work on involved the remaining people in my life that do not exactly meet the standards I am striving toward. One example is family members. By this point in my life journey, I have learned that past comments I made to my parents did not sit well with them or that they did not agree with my choices. I decided to only share information with them that pertained to the conversation at hand, and that would be the extent of the conversation. The rest of the developments that were taking place in my life were shared with those in that sphere of influence.

It was important for me to set boundaries to keep the naysayers at bay and not give them any more fuel than necessary to try to bring me down. I had to practice and be aware of the message I was delivering. None of this was done with malicious intent. It was done to keep myself in development mode and take the risks that would help improve my relationships all around. I had to break away from the old comfort zone that had brought me failed relationship experiences.

Let me give you an example. When I was having discussions with my employer about my transition from the Texas office to the Colorado office, I made the decision to keep it quiet. I knew if I started to tell friends, family, and coworkers about my move that they would not support this exciting life change but would use their energy to make me rethink my move.

For seven months, I kept the whole process quiet. Then the time came for me to announce the move. At this point, I was set firm in my decision and there was no looking back. The news did not go over so well with my tribe. The comments were not 100 percent supportive, but I was so dialed into my life transition that I did not let them hold me down to their standards.

Here are the top three comments that opened my eyes to how limiting people can be when beautiful life changes are taking place:

1. No one drives an SUV in Colorado. (I owned an SUV.)
2. You're from Texas, so you don't know how to drive in the snow.
3. The cost of living in that state is way more than that of living here. You can't afford a fun lifestyle and comfortably live out there.

These are not the types of support statements or relationships I want in my sphere of influence...at all! I thanked them for their concern and comments, but I continued to stand with confidence in my decision. I loved myself so much that I had to let their ignorance die down and follow my own truth.

It's important to build love and trust within yourself so that you can make tough life decisions that resonate with *you*. Sometimes it will feel like you are truly alone, but the aloneness is only for a short moment. When you stand in your own power, the people you start to attract in your life will be in alignment with and supportive of your life standards. Build your muscle of trust.

GOLDEN KEY

Psychologist and relationship expert Dr. Felicia Williams provides the keys to developing self-love. She first became a student of HAI Global, and now she runs workshops for this group alongside Marci Graham (see chapter 8).

Char: What was your personal experience that lead you to discovering the importance of self-love?

Dr. Felicia: I was giving so much to others and not giving enough to myself. I felt like I was missing an element in my life that I was not able to give in my marriage. I was great at giving love to others but missed the self-love piece of being able to receive love.

I fell so hard into give, give, give that I became exhausted and resentful. It was a vicious cycle that my mother did when I was growing up. I had no role model to help me develop my "why" regarding self-care. I was so self-critical that I was running myself into the ground due to lack of self-care. I became physically sick. The best analogy is this: it's like driving a car without any gas in it. It won't move.

Char: How did you overcome this vicious cycle?

Dr. Felicia: I attended a workshop through HAI Global. This workshop showed me the missing link in my life. It was self-love. The process of developing this area in my life has taken time and patience. I am now teaching others how to add this key to their lives through my Self-Love 101 workshop.

Dr. Felicia's Take Action Today

- Bottling up feelings and emotions are detrimental. Allow yourself to experience emotions and feelings.
- Self-love is a foreign language; be patient with this process.
- Take small steps.
- Ask yourself what assumptions you are bringing into a relationship.
- Ask yourself whether you get into a relationship to allow someone to carry the responsibility to love you the way you don't love yourself.

Major Mistake to Face

Oftentimes, we know what is better for the other person, or so we think. It's our ego that gets in the way because it needs to be right.

The choice in this matter is you can be right or you can be in love. When you choose to be in love, it is a signal of self-respect and respect for other people.

<u>Learn to Love</u>
Have an experience of what it's like to be loved.
Be you. Tune in to your heart.
Love yourself for who you are. It's self-full.
This is an inside process.

<u>Dr. Felicia's Resources</u>
Love Yourself to Success
http://loveyourself2success.com/
Love Yourself to Success is born from the principle that working harder no longer gets us "more" and that love is actually a greater motivator than pain.

HAI Global
http://w15.hai.org/
The Human Awareness Institute (HAI) empowers individuals to be potent, loving, contributing human beings. HAI promotes personal growth and social evolution by replacing ignorance and fear with awareness and love.

Six

FINANCIAL THERMOSTAT

You are broke! You are poor! You do not know how to manage money!

The torture we put ourselves through when we talk about lack of money! There is a huge epidemic of a lack of financial education. When money is brought up, people will tiptoe around the issue instead of facing their own beliefs about money. They would rather stare at the issue as if they were staring at a dead rat on the table. They notice this ugly thing, but they don't want to think about a solution if no one else is going to talk about it.

There are some parents who have taken the time to educate their children properly about money and finances. The majority of parents, however, have done an excellent job of feeding their own uneducated beliefs about money to their children. If you are like me, you may have had parents who educated you with:

"Money does not grow on trees!"
"You think I'm made of money?!"
"Don't spend your money! Save it!"

That was about the extent of my financial education from my parents. I carried that with me for many years, as do many other people. You can choose to hang on to false statements, or you can create your own belief system. The financial thermostat from your parents has to be removed in order for you to set your own thermostat. Wake up! Most of our parents were not financial advisors, so why would you continue to trust their belief system and advice about money?

Take ownership in deciding how high you want to set the thermostat. For example, let's say that in the summer, your parents set their thermostat to sixty degrees. Then winter comes along, the thermostat is still set to sixty, and you are freezing your butt off. You do not want to change the setting to a warmer one, though, because your parents always kept the thermostat at sixty degrees all year.

Then you get your own place. Out of habit you keep the thermostat set to the same temperature. Your friends come over; they are freezing and ask you why your temperature is set to sixty when it's thirty degrees outside. You respond with: "That's what I am used to. My parents always had their thermostat set that low. I keep my setting the same as my parents did." Soon enough no one wants to come over because it's too cold at your place. And you are too stubborn to change to a setting that fits you.

That's why you are broke! You have not taken the time to ask yourself what *you* want! Smash that old thermostat setting and change it to suit *your* level of comfort.

MEDIA/SOCIAL STATUS

The media plays a part in helping us determine what wealth and success should look like. People are in a constant frenzy to hold down a job, and they have several credit cards just so they can buy the things that make them look wealthy. Behind the scenes, however, they are hurting from debt, depression, pill addiction, and anxiety.

The stress of trying to keep up with success as portrayed by the media is not a reality for the majority of the population. What you see in the media is only a small percentage of the same usual suspects who are on television constantly. Trying to keep up with a glorified star will only pull you further from your true potential of knowing how to accumulate wealth that is a fit for your life standards.

Take the time to turn off any media and ask yourself some questions around wealth. If there are athletes or singers who inspire you, get to know their stories. Nine times out of ten, they had quite the journey to reach the level of success they have today.

The same goes for social status. You may have friends who appear to be doing better than you, and you envy their lives. Do not get too excited in running a comparison game because you may not be aware of what is going on behind the doors. Some friends are genuinely happy, but they are happy based on their own standards. What are your standards?

FINANCIAL EDUCATION

The financial system is false. If you have not taken the time to do more research on this topic, feel free to look up "fractional reserve banking." So what does this mean? It means that there is no true value to a dollar. There is just a number printed on paper to make it feel valuable, and that is our trade for goods and services. Don't get me wrong; it is very nice to have money to buy goods and services, for sure! Money does make life experiences way more fun. We just need to take the time to gain more education on

- the scarcity effect of money,
- the stock market,
- economy waves, and
- financial advisors.

I used to be guilty of thinking that money is only for the lucky ones, not for someone like me, and that there is not enough to go around. But it became quite clear that my belief system was damaging my potential. I was curious and started wondering if this was true. What makes them different than me? I had reached a point of frustration and really wanted to know what that difference was. During my search, I found that those who were better off than me had passion for what they did, immersed themselves in their work, and were not worried about the idea of a shortage of money. That lack-of-money mind-set was only for those who were lazy about doing the work. The reality is this: there is so much wealth around us, but we have to be in a state of receiving.

The stock market fools those who have not taken the time to read and understand how this business structure works. The mainstream information that is shared displays only the top market movers that are either doing great or crashing. They do not provide information on what is taking place on the opposite side. When one side of the market is moving down, there's an inverse asset that is gaining. But everyone only takes one side of the information and fails to do their own research to see whether there is an opposite side and what that side is doing. This is not advice on what to buy in the market, but it is advice you can use to start asking more questions and taking responsibility to do more research.

The common statement that the economy is going down the drain has been the same for so many years. Yet, how is it, then, that companies are booming and growing every single year? When you raise your level of awareness, you will see the other side of the market that is growing or starting up. This is an area to spend some time in; do not use the excuse that you are not going to do anything until the market turns around. Every time I hear this statement from clients, I have to laugh. It lets me know they are not at a point to take a few minutes to get curious and ask some questions.

Financial advisors can help educate a person on where to invest their funds. I fell into trusting each of my financial advisors on how to invest my money, but when the market fell a few times, they were not quick to advise me to pull my money out of the market to save me from the loss. After this happened to me three times, I was pissed but not at my financial advisors. They were doing their jobs to the best of their knowledge. I was pissed off at myself for not taking the time to educate myself properly about the fund structures they chose to put me in. I did not know which questions to ask my advisors, and I felt trapped.

Something had to change quickly for me. I had to take the time to research, read, and ask questions. I worked with a couple of trading coaches to help me out in the areas in which I was lacking knowledge. Trust me—it was in all areas of my financial investments. I came to a realization: I needed to have the right psychological training to understand that I should treat my investments in the market as a business instead of as a glorified savings account on a slippery slope with penalties.

MONEY AND ENERGY

The constant conflict we fall under is because of our own personal belief system and feelings we have about money. I have heard many people say that money is energy. Everything around us is energy; *we* are energy!

If you go to the gym to lose ten pounds, you have created the idea that it's possible to lose ten pounds. You are inspired to work toward losing that weight by going to the gym, eating healthy meals, and getting proper rest.

It's the same with money. If you want to have more money, you will have to take the action steps to know how much more you want, design a plan to get it, and do what is necessary to obtain it. If you go in with the mind-set that you want to lose ten pounds but do not want to put in the effort to do so, the ten pounds will stick around. If you want to make more money, having a belief system of scarcity and inaction will only make you lose money. Trust me. I made myself an expert victim with my poor belief system around money.

My mind-set had to change, and I had to understand that it is all energy. I fell into the vicious cycle of not allowing myself to receive money. I had an old mind-set and belief system that money and "money-energy" were not for me. It took time for me to build trust within myself, to gain a different perspective and understanding around money, and to take consistent action steps with a new belief system.

Every time I started to fall into the old mind-set, I had to practice shifting to the new belief I was adopting. It felt like a yo-yo emotional struggle at first. I was trying to change something that had been so ingrained in my life since birth, and it took some jackhammering to knock some sense into me. I found that I needed to relax once I got into the flow instead of feeling like I was going to lose all the money in one flash. I used to tell personal-training clients: "It took you time to gain weight. It takes time to lose the weight and get into a new rhythm of a healthy lifestyle." The same applies here for wealth. It takes time to lose an old belief system. It will take time to get into a new rhythm of a wealthy belief system and lifestyle.

CONSISTENCY

Build a plan that will keep you consistent in your wealth flow. I was coaching a few business coaches, and all of them were having their own struggles with their money belief systems. I asked them: "How can you financially grow your clients if you do not trust yourself with your own financial knowledge and set of beliefs?" They were shocked because they had no idea that their financial beliefs were holding them back from growing their clients to the levels that those clients had the potential to reach. Their main concern was to pay down debt. That was it.

They were falling short, however, with a small mind-set around how to use their money. I gave them a few resources on how to leverage money instead of just shoveling it in one direction to pay down debt. It takes consistent action and some financial education to understand how to spread wealth to various areas of your life so that you are not constantly feeling like you are living the dream to only work, pay bills, and get out of debt.

Get going on researching some powerful resources that fit with your lifestyle and the level of success you desire to achieve. Make a simple plan to start with a few dollars a day to track how you are spending, what your mind-set is with spending, and what your mind-set is when you receive money. This awareness will show you where there may be some areas to tweak or overhaul for greater receptivity to wealth.

HAVE FUN

There is plenty of stress in life today, but does it have to be that stressful? When you release that tight controlling grip on your level of understanding about wealth and money, you will start to have some genuine and fulfilling fun in your life.

As a kid growing up in a family of very modest means, I could always tell when my father received his check from work. He had a stern look on his face and would always complain about bills to pay and never having enough money left over to make it to the next paycheck. I took on his energy and thought this is what is was going to be like when I grew up. I honestly thought I had to get into a mind-set of scarcity, fear, and anxiety over what I was paid because it would be ripped out of my hands to pay bills! So I had this idea that it cost a ton to enjoy life and that I could not enjoy it unless I was comfortably wealthy. I was putting undo stress on myself due to an old belief system that I caught from my family as a child.

I had a deep desire to have fun, and I had to find a way to make it happen for me. The day of reckoning came after fighting with myself over a strong, unhealthy belief while I was hiking in the mountains. I realized what I was doing in that moment. I was enjoying the sun, the hike was a healthy challenge, and I felt *great* in that moment. My bank account was not overflowing at that moment, but something else within me was overflowing. It hit me that I had the freedom and choice to enjoy life in this moment and that it was time to relish this wealth.

If you are constantly weighing your level of enjoyment and happiness based on the number that shows on your bank-account statement, you are imprisoning yourself to confirm the old belief system around wealth. Kick it aside and take time to enjoy family, friends, and yourself.

You want to know what true wealth feels like? It feels like the good connections you have with loved ones who make you smile, support you lovingly, and see your truth. That's the long-lasting feeling and effect of wealth. Money is a great tool to create more enjoyable experiences with loved ones.

GOLDEN KEY

Financial expert and friend Trevor Mickelson offers up some key points and resources for not allowing the lack of financial education to hold you back on gaining new insights you can implement today.

Char: What is the top belief you see from clients who are eager to learn more about managing finances?

Trevor: They have a small amount of money for retirement, fly by the seat of their pants, and hope to win the lottery.

Char: How was your financial mind-set developed in your younger years?

Trevor: I was taught to go to college, get a good job, and pay off loans. In college, I took a finance class because debt was building up quickly. The most profound lesson learned in that class was on how to write a check. I thought this was a joke because even college didn't teach me anything that I needed to know about personal finances.

Char: What is your teaching methodology on resetting belief systems on how to manage and use money for long lasting benefits?

Trevor: It comes down to simple basic principles! How much money are you bringing in, what you are spending your money on, what you are saving, and what are some ways to grow your money safely? The majority of people that I meet with don't understand the immense importance of these basic principles, let alone the difference between saving and investing for their future, which could literally be the difference between them retiring in dignity or not.

Many people see money coming in every month and automatically pay their bills, buy food, and so on. People really do not know what they are spending their money on and why. Here's an example: when we pay for services and products, we swipe our credit card for the transaction, and money is no longer tangible.

What I mean is that we are not touching money. We are just seeing what is moving in and out of an online banking account.

I have my clients track their spending by physically writing out what they are spending their money on by listing these transactions on a ledger worksheet.

This exercise removes the "pie-in-the-sky" view that everything will work out all the way to age sixty and then Social Security will kick in in a few more years.

Unless you change something today, nothing will change for you.

Trevor's Take Action Today

- Get a pulse check on where you are today with your finances and your financial belief system.
- Basic education is available (outside of a financial advisor).
- View the last six months for everything you have spent money on. Look at where you can reduce costs and renegotiate service terms (that is, a credit card, cable, Internet, and so on). Small savings really add up!
- Know the direction of where your money is flowing.
- Grow your awareness around your money belief system and money management.
- The millionaire next door was not created over-night. He saved small amounts of money and obtained conservative interest rates over a decent amount of time. It's simple math that makes a huge difference!

Trevor's Resources

360 Degrees of Financial Literacy
www.360financialliteracy.org—Educational site by the AICPA. There's tons of information regardless of what phase of life you are in.

National Endowment for Financial Education
www.nefe.org—Educational site that keeps up with the trends and changes in a changing economy for all phases of life.

The Penny Hoarder
www.thepennyhoarder.com—Fun website that shares ways to earn and save money to get people's heads in the money game.

Feed the Pig
www.feedthepig.org—Education on credit, debt, planning, managing money, and overall financial planning.

Money Chimp
www.moneychimp.com—Great glossary of information, calculators, and overviews of the stock market and Index funds.

Financial Education
www.linkedin.com/in/trevormickelson

Seven

SHATTER THE GLASS CEILING

Having a long-term career in start-up companies and corporate environments trained me to see only the limit of the levels of success tied to my title. When I became an employee of JPMorgan Chase, I was shocked to see how many levels fit within each title. Also, the rules regarding how many levels you were allowed to jump each year before jumping into an upgraded title was ridiculous to me.

For example, if my title was account manager, that title was assigned a number. There were about five levels of numbers within the range of account manager. If I was at the lowest level, I had to patiently wait for that annual compensation review for my manager to determine how many levels I could move up based on my job performance for the year. I had the option to move up two levels at the most because corporate deemed someone not ready to move into a new title unless two reviews were conducted for that person's tenure as account manager.

Being the type of person who does not do well in very defined structures, I had the hardest time adjusting to this process. I also had to wake up! I resolved to never again be in a position that allows someone else to determine my level of growth based on a set of numbers and rules. I made a commitment to never let an organization put me in a system that did not fit with my idea of crushing the glass ceiling.

I started looking at the glass ceiling in all areas of my life: career, education, health, relationships, spirituality, recreation, and community. When I took a deep look, I realized I had a glass ceiling in all areas. Then, I got curious and wanted to figure out where that limit came from and why. The ceilings came from limiting beliefs that I picked up from my sphere of influence.

Articles on the cost of US workplace unhappiness had the following to say:

- *Forbes* (September 2012) reports that "US Workforce Illness Costs $576B Annually from Sick Days to Workers' Compensation."
- A *Business Insider* (November 2011) article titled "14 Surprising Ways Employees Cost Their Companies Billions in the Workplace" reports that
  - stress costs $200–300 billion a year,
  - workplace bullies (from executive level to employee level) cost $16 million in turnover and $8 billion in lost productivity, and
  - smartphones, time wasting, and gossip cost $650 billion a year.

Imagine for a moment if these lost dollars were spent to better your chances of having a career or work environment that brings you true fulfillment. How would this change your limiting beliefs about shattering the glass ceiling?

OPEN YOUR EYES

When I was in my mid-thirties, I was having some health issues. My energy was way down, and I could not understand why I was so tired. I could take a nap for three hours and then turn around and fall asleep for the night a few hours later. In addition, I was running through my monthly cycle every two weeks instead of monthly. I went to the doctor and explained my symptoms to her. She said everything was fine and for me not to change anything I was doing. Six months later, I had another visit with her. She gave me the same response: I was fine. Another six months went by. I asked her to set me up for an ultrasound. She finally complied and scheduled an appointment for me that afternoon.

As I slipped into the other room for my ultrasound, I spoke with the technician about what she was finding.

Me: Do you see anything on the left-hand side?
Tech: Why do you ask about the left side only?
Me: My doctor said there may be something there.
Tech: Honey, you are covered with tumors.

I tried so hard to not lose my cool in that moment. I was livid thinking about the past year of being under the care of a doctor I thought I could trust.

I went home that day feeling betrayed by having put full trust in an expert and assuming I was under a greater level of care than I had been. Instead of dwelling in the emotional pain, though, I quickly started doing some research on options of next steps that I should look into. Some options were extremely invasive, and I did not feel that level of drama would be needed for my condition. I looked into alternative and minimally invasive options that would decrease my recovery time. I was prepared to discuss possible options and next steps with my doctor.

The doctor's nurse called me up two days later to give me their suggestions. She gave me only one suggestion, which was the most invasive treatment option. I asked her about the other options I was researching, and her answer was this: "If you do not want the treatment by the doctor, then you are on your own."

I took her suggestion and went out on my own to find another doctor that would work with me on treatment options. What I found was two years of research and options on how to take care of my body, diet, exercise, and mind-set and how to properly prepare myself for surgery to remove thirteen tumors. I realized the original diagnosis and one suggestion for an invasive remedy was not always the one and only answer.

Just as in the painful herding process of developing my career through levels and numbers based around rules, I felt restricted when I was initially diagnosed. It was irresponsible for me to put full trust in a medical expert who has limited knowledge as well. I had to take responsibility myself and do the research to have better conversations and ask smarter questions. I am grateful today to have found a better doctor, a minimally invasive solution, and a healthier recovery.

This experience led me to open my eyes to all the areas in my life. I needed to examine them and become honest with myself on why I felt there were so many limitations on how far I thought I could go in life. As I started taking the steps toward health and recovery, it was apparent that I owned the choice of what I wanted to accept as realistic and believe when I became aligned with my destined life.

ANCHORS

The anchors that I had been slowly tying to my body were getting too heavy. I was filled with fears of how my life was going to progress as I got older. Was it my destiny to fall into the same patterns and cycles as my parents had, and I was just kidding myself to dare to dream of something bigger?

The anchors I had tied to myself were making me feel worthless and self-pity even though I was driving my life toward results. My mind was in the wrong place. Who was I to dare to jump into new territory that seemed impossible? This kept coming up for me over and over even when I was at the point of starting my own business. I carried those anchors with me and thought I could have a successful business. The universe had other plans for me in starting my business. I had to truly commit and dig to permanently peel the layers and layers of crap that had no use in my life.

Each time I had a personal breakthrough, that glass ceiling was being shattered in all areas of my life. The last glass ceiling to shatter was based on my money mind-set. This one had the ugliest gnarled roots that took some major work. Yours may be something else. You will know which anchor has the most hold on you because it will be the one you struggle with the most as you shatter all the other ceilings in your life. There's always one last piece that needs to be shattered for you to be in alignment with your true destiny.

REALISTIC VIEWS

The realistic levels of growth are up to you and you alone to achieve. It might make you uneasy at first to visualize how far you can take yourself and have the courage to get yourself there. This is important to pay attention to, because the naysayers will come at you with swinging shovels to knock you down and tell you that your goals are not realistic. The only way to shatter the glass ceiling is by seeming unrealistic to those around you and walking in confidence through their unrealistic ideals.

The idea of my divine reality started to take shape when I looked at other successful people actually producing results for themselves, their families, and their communities. My view opened up to a new level of curiosity that made me think and truly believe that if they could do it, so could I.

This was a realistic thought in my head. I was determined to not let it slip away from me due to old thought patterns that got me mediocre results. To play at a larger level, I had to step up and take action at a larger level. I committed to not making excuses for why something did not work. Instead, I made the commitment to ask other questions such as these:

What is my lesson learned here?
What were my mistakes in this process?
What needs to be corrected?
What is my next course of action?

Asking better questions will bring you better results. If someone tried it before you and gave you the idea that it did not work, that does not necessarily mean all hope is lost. Think for a moment how many times in how many years they tested rockets before launching the first rocket into space. Then, they had the knowledge to launch a manned spaceflight years later. They did not end with the idea that if someone failed then it's unrealistic to try. Hell no! They asked questions similar to the ones listed above and kept going.

What are your perceived realistic views that seem to hold you back from raising your standards to a new level of destined reality?

LIMITLESS RESULTS

Wouldn't it be nice to just take that "limitless" pill each day and take charge? You may know this by now, but that pill is not here in this moment. The way to get limitless results in accordance with your destined life is through a newly developed set of beliefs and the willingness to take action.

So far I have mentioned outside resources that have designed rules to keep me from shattering my glass ceiling. The real resource that has the power to shatter any glass ceiling and never look back again is my perception and personally developed reality.

The unrelenting drive for limitless results meant I had to implement my action steps. It's fun to see the idea on paper and research what others are doing, but none of that means a thing unless I do something. I have created, re-created, and reformatted my implementation plan as I've continued to grow. The initial steps I took worked well up to a certain point, but as I grew, a new level of knowledge was needed. I kept getting stuck in the transitions, however. I would fall into the trap of "compare and despair." I was looking around wondering why someone else had had opportunities come their way when they were doing less work. It was constant in every area of my life. Each time this would happen, I had to recollect my mind-set to understand that my journey, my timing, and my opportunity is different. It's hard to see this when you are in the flow of actionable results. I had to stop my action, analyze my frustration and resistance, and reset. These are the stepping stones of life.

The forewarning about limitless results is that you cannot go back to the old patterns of life. The old thoughts may start to creep in, but your action steps are being trained to a whole new level. What happens? A mismatch. When there is a mismatch between the two, you become irritable, frustrated, and uncomfortable. I had a few points at which I was so uncomfortable that I thought about turning back. I was speaking with a mentor of mine about this issue I was having. She laughed at me and said, "You can't go back! It won't work, and you know that. The uncomfortable spot you are in right now is *forcing* you to make a new decision." This is what made me realize that my implementation plan needed to be tweaked to gain a limitless result. It's about constant tweaking!

LOVE

I learned to love and trust myself on a whole new level. When I shattered the glass ceiling in my life, my world was turned upside down. I needed to face the good, the bad, and those dark, ugly spaces that most people would rather cover up with a flowery emotion. Most of the ugly resided in the relationship and financial sectors for me. I started with the fact that I did not have a healthy relationship with myself.

When I was in my early twenties, I was on the phone with one of my older cousins, and she made a comment to me that I held on to. She said, "Charlene, before you get married, get to know yourself first." At that time, I was not quite sure what the full meaning was behind this statement. For some strange reason, however, it resonated with me from that point on. I had to find out why and what this statement meant for me. It was the beginning of a journey to finding my way to falling in love with myself. I figured I owed this much to myself since I was no pro in relationships at all. Why not start with me?

The love and relationship I developed for myself has helped me in determining the essence of the husband that would fit my standards, the business relationships that resonated with me, and the relationship levels between my family and me.

For my health, I have a respect for the high levels of energy that inhabit my soul. When I make choices about which foods to eat, I have the freedom to pick from an assortment of dishes and flavors that nourish my body and soul. Eating for me is like an event. I want to savor every bite and take my time to enjoy the meal. Most people make fun of me for eating so slowly. For example, if it takes most people ten minutes to eat a meal, it's going to take me thirty minutes. I have a love for myself in which I choose to enjoy the moment of eating.

Some people wake up to the truth of being forced into falling in love with themselves, and sometimes that process starts with a very tough circumstance, such as a disease, accident, or obesity. It's better to start your relationship with yourself now than to wait for a challenging life event. Aren't you worth the love you willingly give away to others?

CURIOSITY

The beauty in shattering your glass ceiling allows you to bring out your curiosity. I know I have brought up being curious so many times already, but it makes this process fun. When that ceiling is shattered for the first time in just one area of your life, you are inspired to keep the process going for the other areas of your life. It is only when things get really tough that we lose steam and lose the commitment to keep going forward.

Curiosity helps you push through during those tough moments as well. When you develop a system of asking smarter questions, you begin to steer into the direction that best resonates with your current path. It's a constant movement of taking a different path that produces better results. Stay away from the known path that has continuously brought slim or negative results.

GOLDEN KEY

Relationship expert Marci Graham provides the keys to connecting within. This is an important starting point when we want to shatter the glass ceiling for ourselves. She first became a student of HAI Global, and now she runs workshops for this group alongside Dr. Felicia Williams (see chapter 5).

Char: What was your personal experience that led you to discover the importance of self-love?

Marci: I was in a bad relationship for thirty years, and I needed to know what it felt like to have my own needs considered.

Char: How did you know where to start?

Marci: I attended a workshop through HAI Global. It felt like I found a home in which other people wanted to work on themselves just as much as I needed to work on myself.

Char: What was one of the main realizations you uncovered in learning to love yourself?

Marci: There is no right and no wrong. It kills the spirit when we ignore taking time to develop ourselves and have a relationship with ourselves. Too many people feel guilty and selfish for investing this time in themselves. It's important to love yourself for who you are today.

Char: How do you get people to open up and love themselves?

Marci: The starting point is to check in with yourself. We are in a continuum that is moving so fast. We do not take the time slow down and check in with ourselves. Our body and mind will give us information on what is needed when we are quiet and listen within.

Marci's Take Action Today

- Show up with your truth instead of ego.
- Discuss matters of the heart.
- Be you and allow others to be themselves
- Assumption & Expectations will ambush an experience of what a person can bring to you from moment to moment.
- Know and understand no one is alone in self-loathing or in self-love. It's your choice in where you want to spend your time.

Marci's Technique

- Go inside and explore what is going on inside your body.

- Acknowledge what is going on within you.
- Ask: What do you love about yourself?
- Speak your needs and do not just "think" about them
- The whole body is participating even down to the cellular level when words are spoken.

Marci's Resources
HAI Global
http://w15.hai.org/
The Human Awareness Institute (HAI) empowers individuals to be potent, loving, contributing human beings. HAI promotes personal growth and social evolution by replacing ignorance and fear with awareness and love.

Eight

RE-CREATE

There is an artistic side of life that helps to open up a whole new level of knowledge living inside each one of us. I had no idea how tapping into this treasure would help change my perspective on taking my life to a new platform.

In splitting up the word *re-create*, we are opening doors to new lives for ourselves. It's the same process as reinventing or rediscovering who we truly are. This does not come from the outside. Instead, we are digging deep within ourselves to make our inner expressions come to light. It's *fun* and quite the challenge!

About ten years ago, I took my first painting class to get out of my comfort zone. Let's talk about this for a minute. I have never been formally trained to paint, draw, or think I was artistic. I was uncomfortable with the idea of painting something. But I was committed to throwing myself out there with the ten other people that were in my group. We were taking one of those group painting classes that was instructor led for a specific picture. The goal was to do something fun, release some stress, and be in an environment in which we could laugh, create, and encourage each other.

At first, I struggled. I normally write with my left hand, so it made sense that I would paint with the same hand. When I picked up the paint brush, though, my body instinctively used my right hand. I switched the brush to my left hand and thought I was losing my mind. As I was starting to prep my canvas, my left hand froze, and I could not paint. It felt too awkward. I decided to have some fun with this and tested out the brush in my right hand. Behold! My brain and right hand were on their way to creating something that I had no clue how to accomplish. I was in creative flow!

The painting was completed, and there was a surge of energy running through me. This opened me up in that moment to give myself permission to re-create without applying rules that did not serve me during this creative process.

I would have never come to this realization if I had not allowed myself to paint with my right hand. I would have struggled the whole time just to apply paint to a canvas with my left hand. I would have given up on the process and allowed myself to think I was not gifted to do something that gave me a glimmer of expression with color.

Think about it: how many times do we hold ourselves back due to untrue rules that limit the great potential and value we bring to this life?

PUSHING BOUNDARIES

Our minds will hold us back from stepping into perceived uncharted territory. Then, when we push out of our comfort zone, our brains will throw red flags everywhere and will filter your thoughts to find the imperfections, the ways in which you could fail, and the embarrassment of failing.

The safety net of the mind has its work cut out for it. When you push a small boundary, you are taking the time to retrain and remap the mind to feel the success, the result, and the confidence to stretch out a little more each time. It takes time to learn where you have boundaries set today.

What are some rules you have in your life today that are in direct conflict with the areas of life you would like to experience? It does not matter what level of success you are at today; there are areas in which you continue to hold back. Even considering the tasks and actions you take today, are you really playing at the level you envisioned in your mind? When things are going great, and you are making some progress, that little voice in your mind will pop in to make you question the areas in which you have stretched yourself. This is the point at which people will start to retreat into their old habits and ways of thinking. The commitment to re-create is paramount to being able to face the safety voice of the mind and confidently say, "Thank you. I have found success in trying this out; let's keep moving forward." Your mind will comply, and the anxiety will be removed.

It may seem like a daunting task to push through the comfort zone. There will be people in your life today that will see this shift in you. They will either encourage your transition or try to say things to hold you down.

The first time I decided to go on a vacation by myself, my mother freaked out. I was twenty-five years old and eager to get out of town. I decided to take a little four-day spa vacation to Santa Fe, New Mexico. When I had booked everything and explained my trip to her, she was quick to say, "You cannot go on a vacation by yourself. You don't know what could happen, and you don't know anyone where you are going."

At that time, I thought, maybe she's right. *But* I will not know if I do not go! The trip was set, and I was on a mission to explore a new area. Looking back, I gained more clarity on how she was holding herself back in life.

The first time I ever mentioned moving out of Dallas, I was shocked to hear the response. I was having dinner with a dear couple who were close friends at the time. We were chatting about different areas around the United States to visit. Then, out of nowhere, I heard myself say, "I am moving out of the city and maybe this state someday."

My friends were in shock, and then came the questions:

- Where are you moving to?
- When are you moving?
- Why are you moving? What's wrong with *us*?
- Do you know anyone at the location you are moving to?

It brought me back to the same conversation I had had with my mother years before. I was still in shock, however, at how that statement flew out of me with such conviction. All the questions they were asking me were open for answers that I did not have at that time. The wife of the couple said, "Your friends and family are here. Why would you leave us?"

Again, this was another instance in which I could see how she was holding herself back.

I was open to releasing so much attachment to where I was in that moment and to focusing on where I would like to be. Even though I did not have all the answers to these questions, my action was outside the comfort zones of those around me. I realized that as long as I was staying true to my inner desires I would have to push boundaries for myself. This meant that those who did not see the growth I wanted in my life would inherently fall away as I made more space to surround myself with a different level of resources. It was a challenge at first because I was giving up great relationships, but they were only great for those comfort zones at that time. I noticed, however, that some of those relationships served a purpose at a certain moment of my life.

UNCOMFORTABLE COURAGE

Some people are too scared to take unknown steps outside of their comfort zone unless there is a set step-by-step plan placed in front of them and they already know what the outcome will be. Where's the fun in that?

I was coaching a business professional who did not have much of a passion for the financial role he was in. The only way he would stay in that role long-term was if he was guaranteed a path to move up the ladder. I then asked him what he had a passion for. He gave me two answers on how he would rather spend his time.

Me: "What is holding you back from following one of those choices?"
Client: "I do not want to waste my time doing something in which I do not know the final outcome."
Me: "You want a step-by-step plan laid out before you with the result already provided before you decide your next step?"
Client: "Yes."

He was so terrified of failing, wasting time, and maybe realizing he should have chosen something else. But he was creating a prison by not making a move. Where does that leave him? It leaves him in a dead-end job with no growth and a ton of frustration from not taking action. And all that was because he did not want to be uncomfortable with an unknown result. How many people do you know who are in this space? Or is this you?

Part of growing and raising life standards means having the courage to be uncomfortable. We are the only living species to hold ourselves back from growing. When I look around at nature, animals, and plants, I see an elevated world in which there is life, growth, and death. Not one of them is fighting the natural pattern of life. We are the only ones to fight the pattern.

I was listening to a talk by Rabbi Abraham Twerski on the stress a lobster undergoes when it transitions from one shell to another. The lobster gets to a point of stress, at which it goes into a hiding spot so it can shed the old shell and take the time it needs to grow a larger shell. Imagine the stress it would take on in fighting this progression if it did not shed the shell that no longer fit.

As living souls, we constantly put a crazy amount of stress on ourselves when growth is taking place in our lives due to fear of the unknown. That fear will paralyze you and lead you to a place in which you are in conflict with yourself and those around you. Harness the courage to act in spite of fear.

As we age, fear seems to take over more and more. As children, we are resilient to fear. The only excuse we have between the two are perceived responsibilities that must be handled or else our lives will fall apart instantly. What a lie we tell ourselves. The only true difference that holds adults back more than children is that we have been in the game longer. We have experienced the pain of failure and have realized that we just don't like to fail. Children are new to failing, but they do not see it as failing. To them, it's a game to learn and to perfect. How have we let failure become the wall to put up because we fear the pain? Having uncomfortable courage puts you back in the game of life so that you can build that resilience muscle to failure and move on.

RECONNECT WITH THE INNER CHILD

The process of reinventing or re-creating life should be fun and filled with curiosity. We do an amazing job of taking ourselves too seriously, and thus we miss out on the beauty around us. Why do we find it hard or a challenge to release a genuine smile and laugh heartily?

Years ago, I was in New York consulting with a large financial firm in midtown Manhattan—a great spot for me to people watch. One day I had about fifteen minutes of free time before heading back to the office. I decided to go for a walk and observe life around me. I was looking at facial expressions, body language, and how people were interacting with one another. Here's what I noticed:

- Every person was in a hurry to get somewhere.
- Their faces were so serious with concern over running late.
- People became angry if someone walked in their path.
- Some people had a lifeless stare (zombielike) that poured out misery.

During my observations, I felt sorry for those souls who were so caught up in their own stress. They could not give themselves a few seconds to enjoy being outside or to give a smile to strangers instead of flipping them off out of anger.

We have trained ourselves to take on a level of seriousness that removes the permission to have childlike fun. Who is your inner child, and how do you want to re-create your life to let this child out? Take a chance on tapping in to your inner child, because doing so will open up new ideas, a new perspective, and new options. It is possible to laugh and take care of responsibilities at same time. There are no rules or laws that say you have to choose between fun and responsibility. You can have both.

JUMP

That's right! Have the confidence to *jump*! How many times have you walked up to the edge and then backed down because of fear? What has that cost you? How did backing down make you feel?

The act of jumping brings up a visual of quick movement without hesitation. The commitment to jump takes the courage to believe in yourself. Here's the deal: if you do not believe or trust yourself, who else is going to believe and trust you?

Taking little jumps at a time builds trust within you. It does not make any sense to tell others around you what you are planning to accomplish and then decide to sit back and do nothing. Guess what? The results you are looking to gain from just the idea will be zero. It takes courage to jump into action for some real-life changing results.

COURAGE FOR THE NEW YOU

When I was making the move and driving across the country to a new homestead, my dear friend Mel graciously helped out with the short twelve-hour drive. It was quality time well spent chatting and thinking about the changes to come with my journey to a new state. At one point, she said, "Char, I get this feeling that you are going to have some major life changes."

I thought she was crazy. I had been thinking I would not change much. There is nothing that really needed to change in my life at that point other than the scenery from one state to the next, or so I thought. I had no clue what was about to shift in my life. I realized during that drive that my mind was fearful of the unknown, but I was hungry to step into the unknown.

As I was adjusting to a higher elevation, new work environment, and a new lifestyle, I noticed more questions started coming up for me. These were questions on what I value in life, what type of career I could see myself in for the long haul, and what type of lifestyle change I would like to make for the better. This led me to a whole set of transitions that I had never even thought about.

At the same time, I was excited to see some changes in my life that would lead to more levels of change. It took me some time to gather the courage to take massive action. When I first started talking about these changes, some of my friends did not agree and thought I should just settle down and grow some roots. That was their set of wants, not mine.

I remember I got to the point of telling a few people about me writing a book. This was my first attempt at writing, and I felt that I had a message to share. Then, I allowed a comment from a good friend to make me second guess the book idea. This friend said, "Everyone has a self-help book. Why would you want to make another one just like everyone else? No one is going to read it. I know I wouldn't read another one."

Wow! I realized I had to stop telling others who were not in my new sphere what I was doing. I had to learn to share my dreams and actions with a different crowd. I found a group of helpful souls who had similar characteristics in that they had the courage to separate themselves from the rest their crowd. If I had not created this separation, I would have fallen back to the familiar ground of going back to the same family members and friends who were pushing me down to stay within their comfort zones. I would be in major conflict between pleasing others and pleasing my own drive.

FREEDOM TO LAUGH

We can become too serious on the journey to try something new. I have found myself in the "too-serious" category, and I was not having as much fun as I had hoped for on my new journey. I had to pull myself aside and find laughter to release the undo stress that I was putting on myself.

When I was working through an emotional trigger that no longer served me, I would practice laughing my way into releasing it. Then, I would replace that trigger with something a bit more lighthearted and loving. Let me go back to the comment about my friend talking me out of writing a book. I built an emotional trigger that made me talk myself out of writing a book for a couple of years. The book idea never left me, but I associated a negative emotion with the idea, and I would have this internal conflict that won. I then had to lighten up, face the comment that haunted me, and laugh. After recording about eighty episodes of my podcast show, I realized all of my show notes were actually a book in itself. I had no more excuses and no more fear.

As I started to write this book, the energy and emotion around it was lighter. I found more and more people open to collaborating with me and wanting to be a part of my message and mission. The love that that has poured over to me from others has been truly rewarding.

Take the time to face those fearful triggers that pop up when your heart is wanting you to produce or take action. What can you do to turn it into something more loving and comical for you? Do you have a group or person who will help you stay true to your mission? Have some fun and get curious!

Nine

EMOTIONAL INTELLIGENCE IS SEXY

The whole process and experiences I encountered in my life-development project has led me to believe that emotional intelligence (EI) is key to guiding my moves and reactions.

You see, when we focus on what we do not have, we lose out on the true wealth that surrounds us. It is only when you can get real with yourself that you can develop the level of EI that will get you the results and life experiences that you desire.

What are the benefits of EI?

- You are focused and know what you are going after
- You develop a trusting relationship with yourself that becomes magnetic.
- You set life standards that you will not deviate from.
- You have better financial management skills.
- You have a career that is fulfilling and challenging.
- You take better care of yourself and develop smarter eating habits.

Now if that does not sound sexy to you, I am not sure you will find fulfillment in your life!

BUSY IS NOT WEALTHY

When I am catching up with friends, family, or business associates, I have noticed the following overarching theme:

Me: How have you been?
Them: Oh my goodness! I am so busy! I do not have any time to do anything!

I have been guilty of throwing the "busy" card out there as well. Then I started questioning: what does all this busy-ness truly mean? Are we really getting results, or are we busy trying to run a race that only we are participating in? I have stopped saying I am busy, and here is the way the conversation goes now:

Me: How have you been?
Them: Oh my goodness! I am so busy! I do not have any time to do anything! I bet you are busy too!
Me: No, I'm not busy. I am in flow of getting shit done.
Them: (*No response*)

The dynamic of the conversation has now shifted to having a more impactful discussion. The curiosity kicks in now from the other party, who is interested in knowing what type of results I am getting while they are running around chasing time. I am not sure if others believe the choice of staying busy means being wealthy, but I am sure it has brought me more stress and an almost-bankrupt bank account. I had to shift my mind-set to more focused results and stay away from the busy rat race.

When I was a business consultant to dentists, I would pay attention to the way they treated each patient. When I would show up for a consulting visit, I noticed at the beginning of the day that the doctor was calm and getting into the flow of the daily schedule. All was well. But as soon as something changed in the schedule that caused a little bit of stress, the doctor would lose his cool and change his demeanor to include stressed salutations toward each of the patients for the rest of the day.

As a patient, I would not feel comfortable at all seeing my dentist in a hurry and getting ready to drill on my teeth. No, thank you! Imagine how this impacts business and the retention rate of patients. The doctor's set of excuses for why he was losing patients was blamed on the economy and never on his own reactions to stress. He was too blind to see how wrapping energy around the feeling of "busy-ness" impacted the relationship within the moment. Taking the time to invest in emotional states will release poor excuses.

LOW EMOTIONAL INTELLIGENCE

When someone shows up with low emotional intelligence, the loss of credibility is huge. There are times when I have had to check myself if I am in the wrong state of mind because

I know I am not being fair to the other party in our efforts to bring about a fruitful conversation or result. I feel selfish when I am in the "woe-is-me" mind-set while trying to change lives for the better.

The impact of having a low EI will drive business directly to the other businesses that have the higher EI; it does not matter how many credentials or letters you have behind your name. I have seen many "experts" who claim to be the best at their business, but there is direct conflict between what they say and how they show up. All of the accolades that are written about that person and their business become false to me based on the behavior that I observed. I am not saying you have to show up in your best suit. There is a difference in the truth that is written and what is poured out of the mouth and actions of someone. The deep wells of low self-esteem start to show up when EI is low.

I was once facilitating a two-day workshop for about twenty managers who worked for a financial brokerage firm. This workshop was designed to break down communication walls between these managers and build a collaborative platform for the upcoming year.

One of the exercises was designed to be a challenge with some competitive fun. It also let me see where the shortfalls were in team communication. This exercise provided each team a set of materials and a light set of instructions. The platform was open to allow for creativity and open-minded thinking without the need for a white paper with step-by-step instructions. It was designed to have these managers think outside the box without any repercussions. For an extra challenge, this exercise was timed to see how well this team worked under pressure.

Within the first five minutes of the exercise, one of the managers (we will call her Heather) popped her head up and started looking around the room to see what others were doing and how the other teams were progressing. Immediately, she called me over.

Heather: They are not following the rules!

Me: What rules?

Heather: The rules that you have on the board.

Me: Those are only the basic instructions to get you started.

Heather: That team over there is not following the same way we are doing our project. They are doing it wrong.

Me: What is wrong with their design?

Heather: Look! Their project looks different than my team's.

Me: So what?

By this point, her team was in a frenzy because the original idea was not working out as they progressed into their build. Heather then threw her hands up and started calling each manager's name to see what she was doing.

My observation was that Heather had such a low self-esteem and could not lead or find trust in herself to make decisions for the best. She was too busy trying to set up rules for everyone so the whole group would follow her mistakes. It was quite apparent that she was not of a management caliber to properly lead a team, which showed me where there was break in the flow of the team's structure.

How does this behavior show up for you in projects, communication flow, and interactions with others? Do you let your insecurity take charge during times in which you should show up as a leader?

LISTENING WITH INTENT TO LISTEN

How many times have you been in a conversation but your listening has stopped because you have a response to what the other person said five minutes back and do not want to lose that thought?

Yes, I have been guilty of this! I found that I was the one losing out on listening to the rest of the story. My response was no longer valid because it was a small response to a very small section of the story. I realized I was making people completely repeat themselves due to the ignorance caused by my hurry to respond.

As I have practiced the intention of listening, I am able to remember so much more, and I am present in the moment of the conversation. One day, I was coaching a client, and he asked, "How do you remember everything from the last month of you coaching me? You have been coaching others all day, and you do not write one word down."

I responded with: "I listen!"

That was it; there was no secret to what I was doing. I practiced to listen with the intent to listen and not to respond. I have also practiced being fully present in the moment of the conversation. My mind does not wander off into the zone of what I could be missing out on right now. Instead my mind is relaxed in that moment, knowing I am exactly where I need to be at that time, so I must be in a state of being present.

It has taken me so much practice to be in this state of mind when I am speaking, coaching, or training. For fun, I turned myself into a case study. As I would sit in on conversations, if my mind started to wander off, I had to reel myself back in to the present. At first I would get frustrated with myself for having a "monkey mind," but I had to work on my patience with this too.

I started reading about and researching ways and ideas to help me stay present. I would read a step and then practice, then read, then practice, and so on. The first time I tested out my listening skills, I was headed to Boulder, Colorado, for an interview. I thought I was just meeting with two people that day. I arrived to the office, the assistant sat me down, and she gave me a schedule. I looked, and I said that there were seven names on there. She acknowledged my count and mentioned the eighth person had had to cancel due to a family emergency. Keeping cool in that moment, I said to myself: "How am I going to remember all of these conversations?" My goal was to intently listen.

After the round of seven interviews with no notes, I came back to my hotel and started thinking about the day and conversations. Then, the writing and my notes came. I captured a personal statement about each person, associated it with the picture of his or her face in my head, and then wrote the notes of the rest our discussion. My follow-up emails were on point. I was impressed with myself for practicing this skill because I was fully present the whole day. I was not exhausted from the any of the conversations. I was charged with energy!

IMPACTFUL DISCUSSIONS

As you develop your EI levels, the content of your day-to-day discussions will improve as well. I have had people tell me I am "too businessy" or "straight to the point." Honestly, I have no other way of being, and my discussions are with the right level of people. The ones who say those things about the way I present myself are not at the right levels for me to do business with.

Everyone has their own agenda and an idea of what they want to get out of their discussions. Here's a question: do you value your time and yourself enough to be direct in getting answers? I am sure you would say yes to this question. How are your actions matching what you value?

The development of EI brings you more fulfillment in life. Even something as simple as having a valuable conversation with friends, family, or your husband or wife can help develop your emotional responses.

At first, I found it a challenge to work in this area with family and some friends. It took me about three years to practice my valuable conversations with this group. I am grateful I did not give up even during the times when my family or friends would try to drag me down with the gossip that did not serve me. They know that my time with them is not about gossip but about having a valuable conversation.

HIGH EMOTIONAL INTELLIGENCE

With a high level of EI, I am more focused, driven, ready, and willing to take more leaps in my life. When I think about the last five years, I can clearly see now how much I have developed. Things that would have bothered me are no longer an issue, because I have my sights set on something higher.

Self-confidence and a high EI are two beautiful tools that come with the responsibility to lead and help others around you grow as well. If you are under the impression that no one is paying attention to you, guess again.

I was on the phone with Liz, the mother of one of my friends. It had been years since we had caught up, and she lived across the United States. Then, she made a statement that made me feel happy and showed me that people are watching me to open up their own way to give themselves permission.

Me: It's been so long! Are you doing well?
Liz: Yes! Since I saw you out here a few years ago and you were doing that competition, you have inspired me!
Me: Awesome! I love it!
Liz: No, you do not understand. I have been working out and building strength. I feel stronger and have more energy than I have ever had in my life! Thank you so much!
Me: (*Speechless*)

The impact that my actions had on Liz took her to a whole new level of energy and health for herself. That's just one story of many in which people have come my way and told me how my coaching, training, and podcast shows have left lasting impressions. I am not saying this to brag. This is a statement to wake you up to the fact that through you, others are allowing themselves to go after their dreams too.

Ten

ELEVATE YOUR FOUNDATION

Resistance, frustration, and feeling uncomfortable are signs of growth. It's the actions you take during these growing times that will impact the outcome.

Before I started rocking my own boat of personal development, I had more days of ease and the idea that a simple life was all I needed. Then, new ideas and people started coming into my life to wake me up. I started to realize a simple life was not fulfilling, and there was some major work to do on myself. I kept thinking once I reached this goal, all would be fine and I would not want more. Quite the opposite happened to me. I realized there was more to experience in my life that was bringing me long-lasting fulfillment. The idea of reaching a goal of totality has become my life journey. It was during those times of resistance and frustration that I was being pushed to be more, do more, and receive more.

I had to work on my mind-set during these times of feeling uncomfortable, because the resistance I was putting up kept coming up more and more for me. Within days I would feel like I was settling down to a new comfort level, but then something else would come up to push me just little more. For quite some time, I would fight the growth each time. It was exhausting! I felt like I was starting from the beginning each time. Then, I started to become more alert to the growing pains taking place in my life, and I started to become curious about the lessons I was receiving. I understood that, in order for me to keep moving forward with the mission on my heart, there were going to be more and more days of being uncomfortable. Patience was the key to helping me in this process.

OLD PATTERNS

Some of the thoughts that would consistently come up for me were from the old belief systems I created over the years. For example, when I was in a positive state of mind and taking action, I would feel like I was purposeful with my life direction. Then, when the resistance from growth would creep in, I would find myself thinking along the old patterns that did not fit with my action steps. It's important to catch this as soon as possible to recognize the self-sabotage and correct the thoughts to get back on track.

When the old patterns creep in, it does not mean you are hopeless to fulfill your dreams. It's a sign that some areas need more work. The perfect time to resolve those old patterns is during a time of growth and when you start to put up resistance.

A few practices that helped me included the following:

- getting curious and asking questions;
- recommitting to my vision and becoming aware of any changes that needed to be made;
- reviewing my goals for the current month and looking to see where I have not taken action;
- changing my state of mind by changing the scenery (that is, going for a run) and digging in to the issue (that is, self-analyzing during the run); and
- recharging my belief about who I am destined to become by connecting to my mantra or anchor statement.

ROUTINES

There are times when we have to look at our current daily routine and how much attachment we have to it. When we are elevating our foundation, old routines may no longer fit with the new foundation.

One routine that I held on to for a few decades was having my alarm set each day for the same time. After starting up my own business, I still kept the alarm going as usual. It was a habit for me, and for some reason I thought I would not be able to wake up on time. What I found myself doing for three decades was this:

Alarm goes off at 5:45 a.m.
Snooze for ten minutes.

Alarm goes off at 5:55 a.m.
Snooze for ten minutes.
Alarm goes off at 6:05 a.m.
Snooze for ten *more* minutes.

I fell into the game of snoozing and fighting with my alarm out of a habit that I had mastered for so many years. Then I went out of town for a week and decided to not set my alarm. There were no meetings for me to attend that early in the morning, and I felt I could use some rest. I noticed that that week of no alarm helped me wake up in a pleasant state of mind. *Plus*, I was waking up earlier than before without playing snooze tag with my alarm, and I felt more rested. I realized this was a routine that I could break and reset myself to not feel guilty for not waking up with an alarm.

I began to look into other areas in my life in which routine was an empty habit with no result. I also became curious to look into routines that I would like to implement to bring some new results into my life. For example, I committed to waking up and meditating for about thirty minutes every morning. This practice has helped me to connect with the divine to set my presence for the day. I have found my thoughts and actions to be more focused and the results to be more fulfilling than before. This new routine was in alignment with the elevated foundation I created. By giving myself permission to change and try on new routines, I am able to make adjustments that resonate with the changes in my life.

CONSTANT DEVELOPMENT

The thought of constantly developing yourself can seem like a daunting task. Think about it. We are always developing ourselves each day, so it should not appear to be a daunting thought or task. That's when laziness kicks in, and the adult temper tantrum ensues.

One of my high-end consulting clients on Wall Street loved the software system they were using to track their portfolio structures. When he moved to another firm, they ended up using the same software system but with more user functionality. I was brought in to provide more training on the software system for him and his group. When I saw him, he was beyond excited and could not wait to learn more about the system. He had more power at his fingertips than he did when he used the system at his previous firm.

The third day I was there, he came up to me in pure frustration, threw his hands up, and said, "I can't do this! I don't understand how to work the system! This is a waste of time!"

My first thought when I saw this reaction was, Grow up! I was shocked to see a knowledgeable professional turn into a three-year-old child because he was uncomfortable with learning something new. As soon as something became a challenge, he resisted and decided to put up resistance to the growth. The downside to this behavior was that he was not willing to open himself up to more development.

How many times in our lives do we ask for more, and then when we get it, we fight and resist because we are being challenged and stretched?

It is important to be flexible with ourselves during this process. We should be open to making mistakes and admitting it if something does not make sense. When we let go and open up to the development taking place, we can become more curious about options, openly ask more questions, and view new directions to elevate ourselves to a new level.

When I started my journey of setting up my business, I was completely clueless about what I was really getting into. There were so many programs and seminars that I listened to or attended. These programs were designed to show me a possible way to success without making the same mistakes the trainer or speaker had made during his journey, but the catch was that I had to follow that person's system. I ended up making many of my own mistakes. There is no fail-safe system that is out there.

I realized I had to take the information I was receiving, adopt what worked for me, and be open to making my own mistakes. This is a huge part in the development process. We get a choice: take on the risks, bumps, and bruises that come with development or suffer from the tantrums in fighting the development process and go crazy from fighting with yourself.

NEW DIRECTIONS

Release the fight when you are trying to elevate your foundation. We all have a desire to have more exciting experiences in our lives, to build closer relationships, and to have more success. The only way to get these things is by taking on new directions that you may not have realized were available to you.

Some major life changes kicked into high gear when I started working with a business coach, a life coach, and a spiritual healer at the same time. I chose to work with coaches due to the fact that I needed help in sorting through the current belief systems that were holding me back. I knew if I was serious about making some major changes in my world that I needed to ask for help from the right people. I made it a point to not reach out for help from family or friends because none of them were at the levels that I was looking to reach. Actually, most of them believed it was unrealistic for me to take the chances that I was craving to take.

I understood that they would step in if I had been taking chances that would have possibly harmed my physical and mental well-being. But the chances and directions that I was moving into were so foreign to family and friends that they had no idea how to provide support. What little advice they tried to offer did not match the level of growth I was seeking. This is where I had to tap into other experts who were in my field of interest and ask for their advice.

As you take on new directions, seek out those professionals, mentors, and experts who will guide you along the way. Beginning to change your life direction is not a task that you should feel alone in doing. Find ways to surround yourself with others who are like-minded.

RISK, TRUST, LOVE
Take the risk to trust and love yourself on this life journey!

Most people will duck and hide from taking any risk. Why? Because they have seen pain associated with taking risk. Who wants pain?

When I speak of taking the risk, I mean that you should take the risk to trust and love yourself. If there are events and actions that have left you feeling guilt and regret, face those feelings and pour your love over them.

I have had the chance to get to know some amazing and extremely wealthy individuals. How they appear on the outside and how they show up to the public makes people think that these individuals have it all. But behind closed doors they are working on themselves too. Drop the comparison game, drop feeling like you are not worthy of love, and drop the hate you have placed on yourself.

Take the risk to step in to who you are today and ignite your path to who you wish to become. This whole book is a resource to drive you to your own inner truth by building trust and learning to truly love. The one person to start with is *you*.

- You are the only person who can take the steps.
- You are the only person who truly understands you.
- You are the only person to make the choices.

The beautiful result is being able to share yourself more openly, have confidence, have more trust, and willingly love others more easily.

When I recommitted to writing a book, this book specifically had my mind chatter going in my head. The chatter was saying, "You didn't complete your other three books. What makes you think this is the one to complete?" I knew that voice was speaking truth to me regarding my prior commitment. But I had to change my mind-set, move through what had happened in the past, and resolve myself to make it happen. I am grateful and thankful to have developed a relationship with myself in order to have the courage to move forward.

It was not an easy task to develop trust with my stubborn personality. There were so many times when I had to check and release my ego when it started to well up. I had to redirect my energy into a state of love to be able to move past the point at which I had given up, and I had to redirect my attention to allowing myself another shot at writing a book.

There are many areas in which we have fallen over and over again and feel like it's useless to give ourselves another chance. How about those times when you start a diet, and a few days later the ego gets in there and tells you to give up like all the other times? It's not a lost cause to want or to try to be healthy. Your trust and love for yourself must be built to a strong level to overcome the noisy ego. *Give yourself another chance*!

MAN UP

It's wasted energy to spend time comparing yourself to others and making yourself feel worthless. Shift the energy to learning how to become better than who you are today. Spend time researching role models who resonate with your value and belief systems. Allow any naysayers to take a backseat while you redirect your energy and time to reinventing your life. Feel free to reinvent yourself as many times as you need to. Oprah Winfrey reinvents herself constantly.

We spend so much time throwing emotions away to jealousy, envy, anger, hatred, and frustration toward others for no reason. Imagine spending one full day shifting those emotions to happiness, love, confidence, gratitude, and being vulnerable toward yourself.

The time has arrived! This is your chance to harness courage to live a destined life that will

- elevate life experiences,
- bring fulfillment and happiness in all you do,
- ignite love and trust with no boundaries, and
- build long-lasting relationships.

APPENDIX: SELF-ANALYSIS

Take some time to think about the actions you take today. What is the basis of those actions and where were they initiated? That is, are your actions inspired by you or someone else's desires? Write out your answers to the questions below. Visit www.wakeupbreakrules.com to download the Self-Analysis worksheets.

What are some beliefs that led your actions today?

_____

_____

_____

_____

_____

_____

Where did those beliefs come from (family, friends, teachers, media, and so on)?

_____

_____

_____

_____

_____

_____

How do those beliefs serve your life today? For example, do you have confidence to grow, do you feel stuck in life, are you waiting for the right time to make some big positive life changes, and so on?

_____

_____

WAKE UP! BREAK RULES!

From your earliest childhood memory up to today, list your top ten to twenty empowering life experiences. On a scale of 1–10 (1 = low, 10 = high), rate your level of passion and level of fulfillment for each experience.

Empowering life experience	Level of passion for achieving success in this experience	Level of fulfillment/ satisfaction

WAKE UP! BREAK RULES!

If you answered an 8 or below, write out why you feel this empowered life experience(s) did not bring a higher level of fulfillment in your life.

_____

_____

_____

_____

_____

_____

Write out ten to twenty life experiences that were at full level-ten energy. What event or experience happened in which this level-ten energy was hijacked (for example, death of a loved one, rage, fear of success, traffic jam, demeaning comments, and so on)?

Level-ten life experiences	Event that hijacked your level-ten energy

Write out what you felt in reaching success and having a heightened level of energy.

What must you do to create more passion and life-fulfilling experiences on a consistent basis? Oftentimes we get stuck in believing that our past will not allow us to have a better life today. Release this anchor and believe you can shift into a happier life. Think of all areas of life: relationships (with yourself, family, friends, business associates, and so on), career, finances, health (spirit, mind, and body), community, and continued learning.

Write out actions you must implement to bring fulfillment in each of these areas.

_____

_____

_____

_____

_____

_____

_____

_____

_____

_____

_____

_____

_____

_____

_____

<u>Leverage support</u>. When it comes to transitioning into a life of taking on full responsibility in raising the bar on life experiences, it's important to identify people and resources that can help support you on this journey. Make a list of those who will help you.

Friends:

Family:

Business partners/associates:

Groups/organizations/advisors:

Resources/educational research:

<u>Connect and engage</u>. Be clear on how this person or resource can help you. Do your research, ask specific and smart questions, and be curious.

What areas would you like help with?	Who is the best person or resource to advise you?	What is your level of commitment to finding the answer that resonates with your inner truth?

Break rules!

ABOUT THE AUTHOR

Charlene is dedicated to the concept that development is both a business tool and a life tool. As a strategic, visionary thinker, she has a passion for inspiring people at all levels to optimize their full potential while maintaining a focus on living a balanced life.

She has had the privilege of leading her audiences though the processes of understanding the human condition, revealing that the true key to influence is through an intelligence that inherently brings an understanding of what people want, what they truly value, and how that impacts building strong relationships based on a mutual agreement of accountability and success.

Charlene brings the business experience gained from a career in the financial-services industry, working for such companies as JP Morgan Chase and Markit, where she built, developed, and led a variety of account management and operations teams charged with servicing accounts with $500 million–$20 billion in assets.

Charlene is a business consultant, speaker, and podcaster.

For further information, contact www.execedgeworks.com.

33538227R00081

Made in the USA
Middletown, DE
17 July 2016